Contemporary Classics of Children's Literature
Series Editor: Morag Styles

Frightening Fiction

Contemporary Classics of Children's Literature

Series Editor: Morag Styles

This exciting new series provides critical discussion of a range of contemporary classics of children's literature from Britain and elsewhere. The contributors are an international team of distinguished educationalists and academics, as well as some of the foremost booksellers, literary journalists and librarians in the field. The work of leading authors and outstanding fictional texts for young people (popular and literary, including media texts) is considered on a genre or thematic basis. The format for each book includes an in-depth introduction to the key characteristics of the genre, where major works and great precursors are examined, and significant issues and ideas raised by the genre are explored. The series provides essential reading for those working at undergraduate and higher degree level on children's literature. It avoids jargon and is accessible to interested readers such as parents, teachers and other professionals. Contemporary Classics of Children's Literature is a pioneering series, the first of its kind in Britain to give serious attention to the excellent writing being produced for children now.

Also available in the series:
Kate Agnew and Geoff Fox: *Children at War*
Nikki Gamble and Nick Tucker: *Family Fictions*
Peter Hunt and Millicent Lenz: *Alternative Worlds in Fantasy Fiction*

Contemporary Classics of Children's
Literature

FRIGHTENING
FICTION

*Kimberley Reynolds, Geraldine Brennan and
Kevin McCarron*

CONTINUUM
London and New York

Continuum
The Tower Building   370 Lexington Avenue
11 York Road   New York
London SE1 7NX   NY 10017–6503

© 2001 Geraldine Brennan, Kevin McCarron and Kimberley Reynolds

First published 2001

British Library Cataloguing-in-Publication Data
A catalogue record for this book is available from the British Library.

ISBN 0–8264–5309–0 (hardback)
    0–8264–4976–X (paperback)

Typeset by YHT Ltd
Printed and bound in Great Britain by TJ International Ltd, Padstow, Cornwall

Contents

Acknowledgements

Some material in the Introduction first appeared in J. Webb (ed.) (2000) *Text, Culture and National Identity in Children's Literature*. Helsinki: NORDINFO.

Some material in Chapter 1 first appeared in G. Avery and K. Reynolds (eds) (1999) *Representations of Childhood Death*. London and New York: Macmillan.

[KR] For my mother, in memory of Tall Jane

[GB] For MaryClare

[KM] For Ella and Max

Introduction

Kimberley Reynolds

The commodification of horror

Over the last two decades books marketed with the promise of providing a frightening experience, usually involving the label 'horror', have spectacularly dominated children's publishing, making fortunes for individual writers and significant profits for publishing firms. Particularly active in the UK and USA is Scholastic, publisher of the prolific R. L. Stine, author of the best-selling GOOSEBUMPS books and many titles in the most influential series, Point Horror. With cumulative sales of Point Horror titles currently standing at 6.9 million,[1] the series contributes substantially to the company's profits and has made it the market leader in the world of frightening fiction for young readers in the UK. Not surprisingly, many publishers have produced copycat series, hoping to cash in on the Point Horror bandwagon, which means that currently young people in the UK can feed their appetites for what they refer to as 'horror' by choosing from a large number of series, including 'Nightmares', 'Horroscopes' and, for younger readers, GOOSEBUMPS.

Adult reaction to the sales of texts promoted as 'horror' has been mixed. Publishers and booksellers naturally welcome the boost to sales and revenue, and many parents and teachers are pleased to see children buying, borrowing and *reading* books, whatever their provenance. But other groups are less sanguine. While no bill has been rushed through Parliament banning the new wave of horror novels, as happened in the 1950s when groups headed by the Comic Campaign Council vilified horror comics as 'symptoms of a moral and spiritual sickness',[2] anxieties have been expressed about the potentially harmful effects on young people of getting the horror habit. When they first appeared *The Daily Telegraph* branded books in the Point Horror series 'vile and truly pernicious'; though seemingly less critical, *The Observer*'s observation that 'there are worse things to be hooked on' went on to associate a taste for Point Horror with a propensity for substance abuse. Meanwhile, the Campaign for Real Education insisted that 'These books should not be given the space that "good" books used to have.'[3] As Kevin McCarron discusses in Chapter 1 of this study, comparison of the charges levied against the books and the books themselves suggests that many of those who decry Point Horror and its textual clones apparently turn very few, if any, pages of the books before making pronouncements about them. Instead, the label 'horror' is sufficient in itself to render the books suspect.

Concern about the effects of reading 'horror' stems from the fact that as a genre, it tends to be associated with kinds of knowledge and forms of experience regarded by many as unsuitable for children, notably those involving the occult or provoking high levels of fear or anxiety. In fact, anyone who reads widely in the current wave of juvenile and adolescent 'horror' fiction will recognize that publishers apply the label very loosely and frequently inaccurately, largely for the purposes of increasing sales. Whereas traditionally horror has been characterized by the drive to leave readers feeling uneasy and fearful in the face of uncertainty – Did the events really happen? Could they recur? Has the threat been vanquished? – much of the fiction now sold as horror and written with a juvenile audience in mind is notable for the sense of security it ultimately engenders. Instead of ambiguous endings, the closure of these novels is typically a disclosure in which what was thought to be inexplicable is explained, and what seemed dangerous and menacing is made safe and often even comfortable. And the younger the intended audience the stronger the drive to take the horror out of horror fiction. Extended reading throughout the range of texts currently available shows that publishers are producing very different kinds of horror texts for different age groups. Classic horror, the kind of text that creates powerful feelings of disgust and uncertainty, tends to be directed at an adult audience. Although such books are also read by young people, their celebration of violence, gratuitous inclusion and lingering over horrific incidents, delight in social anarchy and glamorization of outsiders is quite unlike the majority of texts produced with an adolescent audience in mind. While adolescent horror generally involves plots designed to make readers believe terrible things are going to happen (as indeed they sometimes do), overall, horror fiction directed at young teenage readers backs away from the uncertain endings or all-pervasive sense of fear and ghastly transgression which characterizes true horror. Far from delighting in the attractions of misfits and outsiders, adolescent horror is concerned with instilling a desire to belong to recognized social groups, teaching readers how to behave in ways which will make them acceptable rather than monstrous. The *modus operandi* is still fear, but it is fear of the consequences of behaving in other than conventional and acceptable ways. Ultimately most adolescent horror texts promise that those who conform will be accepted, happy and at ease with themselves.

The most recent manifestations of horror from children's publishers have been aimed at readers as young as six or seven years of age. Though such texts imitate the narrative voice associated with traditional horror – strong on suspense, intimating impending crisis, trying to create a sense that something dreadful is just about to happen – they are in fact primarily concerned with showing many childish fears to be unfounded. Imagined monsters and dangerous strangers turn out to be perfectly ordinary objects and individuals, and such books tend to be punctuated with explanations of how the mistaken perceptions came about. This may be a conscious strategy for reassuring and empowering children at a time when British culture has a highly developed sense of the possible range of dangers to children. (Interestingly, at the time of writing, a conference of scientists at the University of Sussex warned parents of the social and health problems created by raising children in a 'culture of fear', which prevented children from such basic freedoms as unsupervised play and travelling to school independently.[4]) However, the certainty and sense of control produced by such texts are precisely the opposite of the reactions inspired by horror, or any other kind of fiction designed to create a feeling of fear in readers. For that reason examples of such texts are not discussed in this study.

Although inaccurate, the strategy of grouping many kinds of texts and genres under the label 'horror', and frequently changing the overall nature of the experience from disquieting to reassuring, works in commercial terms. It seems that writers, editors and publishers have identified and succeeded in satisfying a taste among young people for narratives which evoke, but then generally dispel, bizarre, frightening and/or inexplicable events. The result is a hybrid genre, which masquerades under the label 'horror', but which in reality combines characteristics of what literary critics have traditionally termed the fantastic, the marvellous, the grotesque, the Gothic, the uncanny, literature of terror, and literature of the occult.[5] Many books that include the word 'horror' on their covers in fact make use of none of the traditional features of horror fiction. Instead, they could more accurately be described as suspense or psychological thrillers. Such generic niceties are less important to this discussion than arriving at an understanding of the vogue for frightening fiction. The seemingly insatiable demand for it suggests that, at least for the moment, it satisfies a narrative need in many young people.

The purpose of this study is accordingly threefold: to identify the dominant characteristics of what is effectively a new genre of 'frightening fiction'; to investigate its appeal to young people, and the commercial response to that appeal, and finally to consider its possible use by and effects on readers. It is important to investigate both the literary and the commercial aspects of the phenomenon, for as the cultural critic Joseph Grixti observes:

> the fact that the contemplation of horrific[6] eventualities has become an expanding industry with apparently vast investment potential raises important questions about the types of societies in which we live, and also about the manner in which our methods of developing fictions to help us make sense of experience have become inseparable from the demands and complex orientations of consumerism.[7]

In the following chapters the work of six very different but equally interesting writers will be discussed. At the opposite ends of the literary spectrum are David Almond, whose books have recently attracted positive critical attention and some major children's literary prizes, and R. L. Stine, best-selling Point Horror and GOOSEBUMPS writer. Stine has won no prizes, but with sales of 10.5 million GOOSEBUMPS titles alone,[8] his books have probably been read by more children than any other contemporary writer, with the possible exceptions of Roald Dahl and J. K. Rowling. The work of Stine's Point Horror stablemate, Caroline B. Cooney, is used to complete the profile of this most popular of the juvenile series which exploit the narrative attractions of fear. In the concluding chapter, Geraldine Brennan sets David Almond's work alongside that of Philip Gross and Lesley Howarth, two challenging writers who have produced examples of frightening texts that extend the normal definitions of horror or conventionally scary tales. The trio provide a good overview of the way writers are using fear to deal with important issues in contemporary society. The final featured author is

Robert Westall, whose substantial and eclectic *oeuvre* often explores the boundaries between the normal and the paranormal, the safe and the unsafe, the psychotic and the misunderstood. Westall enjoyed considerable critical success in his lifetime, and his novels and short stories have commanded a dedicated readership over a number of years. Indeed, rather appropriately given the genre under consideration, he seemed for a time to continue to write from beyond the grave, with posthumous publications appearing for several years after his untimely death!

The work of these writers provides a good cross-section of the forms frightening fiction has taken in recent years, and through a combination of close reading and cultural analysis of selected texts by each it is possible to draw some conclusions about the nature of these narratives.

Functions of fear

The fact that four of the six writers discussed are male is not accidental; currently the best-known writers of frightening fiction are men. However, in the past similar kinds of texts tended to be produced primarily by women. In *Our Vampires, Ourselves*, Nina Auerbach goes so far as to claim that 'in the eighteenth century horror was *by definition* a woman's genre', though it is widely rejected by women writers today[9] (my emphasis). How do we account for this change in production? Does it also suggest a change in audience? In Chapter 2 of this study Kevin McCarron discusses gendered responses to horror and explores the possibility that today a peculiarly male form of horror/frightening fantasy has emerged in tandem with youth culture's male rebels and the rejection of the cosy domestic world fetishized in the books, radio and television programmes of the postwar period.

The fact is that at least since the 1950s and the vogue for American horror comics, many young people of both sexes have actively sought narratives, both in print and on the screen, that include and may even primarily be about incidents which combine horror, violence and the supernatural. A number of theorists have attempted to explain this predilection, especially among adolescents. For instance, according to J. A. Appleyard, it stems from the fact that:

> Teenage readers have discovered that the conventions of juvenile literature do not match the complexity of their new experience. And as a result they demand that stories not just embody their wishes and fantasies, but also reflect realistically the darker parts of life and the newfound limits on their idealism.[10]

Specifically, Appleyard is alert to the way that the element of horror in these texts frequently functions as a metaphor for the experience of change and separation characteristic of adolescence and the growing sense of 'a split between the "me nobody knows" and a changing personality'.[11] Similarly, when discussing fantasies which present the self as split between the benign familiar and a hostile/aggressive other, Rosemary Jackson explains this as a manifestation of alienation, the consequence of a period of libidinal drive during which fantasies compensate for society's prohibitions by allowing vicarious fulfilment.[12]

Both Jackson and Appleyard offer well-rehearsed psychoanalytic explanations for adolescents' attraction to narratives that deal in disturbing images and events. Such texts, the argument runs, mirror maturing children's recognition that the world is not always such a pleasant place as they may previously have been led to believe, and this feeling is corroborated by the fact that they themselves have feelings and drives that sometimes seem strange, overwhelming and threatening. As has long been recognized, the image of monsters, aliens, or other kinds of supernaturally powerful beings who take over the body of an ordinary person (a frequent motif in conventional horror and one which is used regularly in contemporary forms of frightening fiction) provides the perfect metaphor for this stage in a young person's development. Through it 'the beast' many teenagers suspect they harbour within themselves can be externalized, encountered and finally overcome.

This kind of explanation, however, provides only a partial understanding of the complex nature of the appeal of such texts, and risks treating them as if they all provide the same, ultimately cathartic experience. Moreover, in focusing on the emergence and demands of sexual drives in adolescents, it ignores other possible ways in which such narratives tap into and shape young people's views of the world. A critic who takes a different though also largely psychoanalytic approach to analysing the appeal of horror is Julia Kristeva. In *The Powers of Horror: An Essay on Abjection* she explores why readers of any age seek out the feelings of disgust or loathing typically encountered in texts which employ the modes of horror. According to Kristeva, this urge stems from the need to reinforce the transition from what she terms the maternal *semiotic* realm to the paternal *symbolic* realm, begun through processes such as weaning, toilet training and the entry into language. While the mother/infant relationship of the semiotic phase is a symbiotic one, outside the demands of civilized society and characterized by connection based in shared bodily rhythms and sensations, the symbolic belongs to the civilized social world and the

autonomous individual. Entering the symbolic is achieved at a cost –
the separation from the blissful condition of unity with the mother –
and maintained with difficulty. This means that anything which
threatens to undermine the self-identity achieved by the transition to
the symbolic is construed as fearful, and images associated with the
domain of the semiotic come to be regarded as loathsome and
repugnant. Following Kristeva's logic it is not surprising that many of
the images employed in frightening fiction are connected with the
semiotic. Think, for instance, how many monsters are inarticulate,
infantile in their constant demands which can never be met, and leak
bodily fluids like an untrained infant.

Kristeva's explanation is helpful to understanding the images,
vocabulary and functions of frightening fiction: 'anything that
threatens to send the subject back into the semiotic is accompanied
by sensations of dread' and provokes the urge to re-enact and so
reconfirm the transition to the symbolic.[13] The images that frighten us
are perverted and disguised images of what we long for, perhaps
especially during the turbulent years of adolescence when the process
of separation begun in infancy is generally reactivated: a return to the
sense of complete and satisfying connection of infancy. Since this state
can only be achieved through regression and ultimately the destruction
of the self, it must be vigorously rejected and its appeal denied.

The destruction of the self seems always to be immanent in
frightening fiction. While Julia Kristeva explains the feeling of loathing
stimulated by horror as a response produced by the need to reject the
seductive and ultimately destructive appeal of the semiotic, feminist
critic Helen Cixous understands fascination with the bizarre and
uncanny, equally common in such narratives, rather differently. It is,
she says, 'not merely ... displaced sexual anxiety, but ... a rehearsal for
an encounter with death'.[14] Flirting with the idea of death can be
understood as the beginning of accepting that death is inevitable, an
idea which is beyond most young children. At the same time,
adolescents frequently believe (or act as if they believe) that they are
immortal. Texts which provide vicarious encounters with ghosts, the
undead, and others who exist outside the conventional definitions of
life may be read as confirming this belief: seeing a ghost is frightening,
but it can also be taken as evidence that death is not the end of the
self, and even that interaction with the known world remains possible
after death.

As they move into and through adolescence young people are often
required to take chances, make decisions and evaluate risks.
Accordingly, texts that are preoccupied with these processes, and in

the case of frightening fiction often present them in terms of extreme situations with exaggerated consequences, are understandably interesting to the adolescents whose anxieties and feelings they may reflect. When everything seems to be in flux and yet the responsibility of the individual, rules and boundaries may be welcomed in a way not usually associated with adolescence. But you can only rebel against rules that have been identified, and according to Charles Sarland, whose *Young People Reading: Culture and Response* provides an in-depth study of a group of young people's readings of texts that can be classified as 'frightening fiction', an important part of the appeal of works that deal in violations of acceptable behaviour and transgression of norms is their ability to identify precisely the kind of rules and boundaries that define acceptable behaviour in our culture:

> In the social construction of reality that culture is, it is necessary to learn the boundaries of cultural order, and to learn what those boundaries are it is just as necessary to learn what is beyond them as to learn what is within them. In the learning process, then, the concept of the cultural 'other' is crucial ... for identify[ing] and question[ing] those boundaries.[15]

Thus, and perhaps surprisingly to the critics of 'horror', one effect of reading frightening fiction is likely to be the reinforcing of the status quo. By putting normality in jeopardy, it creates a desire for its return and future security.

Of course this is not what most young people think they are doing when they read frightening fiction, and especially when it is packaged under the label 'horror'. Despite the often conservative drive embedded in such texts, the act of choosing, circulating, reading and relishing such texts is oppositional. As reactions to Point Horror show, for the most part, adults neither approve of nor appreciate it. This may be particularly true of the current generation of parents of teenagers, many of whom grew up in the 1970s when peace, pacifism and pro-civil rights activism were youth's weapons against the adult world of the military-industrial complex. To them the racist and sexist overtones of the violence and threatening situations frequently associated with the genre are peculiarly offensive. But it is worth remembering that in the adult-controlled world of books, it can be difficult for young people to find ways of defining themselves against the dominant culture's values with which books and the act of reading tend to be closely associated. Juvenile novels which advertise their ability to frighten and shock can have this effect on some adults; narratives that make use of occult or supernatural elements for their effects increase the opportunity for adult disapproval among certain groups. Young people, and especially adolescents, are looking for agency, the acquisition of power that will enable them to make decisions and operate effectively in the world. While they are young and so lacking in political, economic and social power, it is often only by stepping outside the dominant ideology that they can achieve this sense of agency. Finding alternative, oppositional positions from which to assess past and present generations is a necessary and valuable part of the work of growing up. Frightening fiction can play a part in this process, and though this is unlikely to be a conscious reason for reading on the part of young people, it may nevertheless contribute to its appeal.

According to Sarland's study, for girls especially the act of reading certain kinds of fiction seems to have the potential to intensify their sense of agency and control. When Sarland was conducting his research, adolescent 'horror' was less widely available than it is now, so most young people who chose to read frightening fiction had to find what they wanted among books published for an adult audience. The two books chosen by the students who participated in the project were *First Blood*, the first Rambo story, and Stephen King's *Carrie*. Both books are more violent, and in the case of *Carrie* more frightening, than is typical of adolescent horror and other kinds of frightening fiction, potentially giving them added value in the oppositional stakes since, according to traditional constructions of femininity, girls 'aren't supposed' to like violence. That girls *do* choose to read and to be seen to be reading such texts is underlined by responses to a survey of nearly 9000 young people undertaken by the National Centre for Research in Children's Literature. For instance, one of the five most popular authors with 11–16-year-olds was R. L. Stine, named by 410 respondents, only 78 of whom were boys.[16] It's worth thinking about the appeal of such texts for girls, given that at the older end of the spectrum in particular the subject position many of them seem to offer young female readers is that of the victim or potential victim – as objects of desire, obsession and revenge.

Sarland's work suggests that young people not only read differently from adults – that texts are not only constructed and reconstructed across generational lines – but also that socio-sexual differences may result in boys and girls reading the same texts in different ways. Sarland's findings largely confirm other studies into gendered responses to reading: he concludes that girls tend to read in ways which emphasize emotions and affective relationships, while boys focus on action and information. What is particularly interesting about his findings, however, is that that he observed girls applying their reading strategies to texts that seem to preclude them. For instance, even in *First Blood*, a text characterized by action, aggression, and lack of significant women, he found girls' narrative satisfaction came from reading the story in a feminine way. They were interested not in what the characters *did*, but in what motivated them to do it. When discussing the book his girl readers highlighted such things as implied relationships, body language, and contradictory behaviour to construct sympathetic explanations for violent acts.

Given what we know about the gendering of the reader, this way of reading is not surprising. However, Sarland observed another way in which girls resisted the male-dominated ideology of the novels which suggests that, consciously or not, they were reading against the grain of the texts and refusing to accept the version of the world they offered. Rather than finding the texts they read frightening, the girls tended to find them amusing, and especially so 'at points of maximum male sexual assertion'.[17] This group of girl readers regularly reconstructed scenarios in which aggressive male sexuality and power 'should' have intimidated them into scenes which exposed the inadequacy they interpreted as provoking excessive displays of machismo. As a consequence, instead of positioning themselves as victims in these texts, girls found reading them empowering.

Following on from Sarland's work on female responses to frightening fiction is the possibility that for some girls, raised at a time when feminism has become a new kind of orthodoxy, it offers ways of negotiating current constructions of the 'right' way to grow up female. Reading outside the range of books approved by parents and educationists is a well-established form of subversive activity for young women. It gives the appearance of conforming to traditionally acceptable female behaviour: for the most part it takes place indoors (many male forms of rebellion and manifestations of sub-cultural activity are enacted on the street), is internal, private, and requires no physical exertion. Though reading gives the appearance of passivity, the effects of taking on board new stories, vocabularies, metaphors and ways of thinking can be explosive. This is especially true now that new images of females are being incorporated into such narratives – images that combine the stereotypical elements of the physically attractive and desirable young woman (attributes frequently scorned by feminists) with academic, social and physical powers traditionally associated with male heroes.

A new and as yet little-known and incomplete series by Francine Pascal (author of the remarkably successful 'Sweet Valley High' series) features a paradigmatic new female hero in its central character, Gaia

Moore. Gaia is not only drop-dead gorgeous (though like many a modern girl she has a terrible body image), she's also a genius, trained in the martial arts, and born without the gene for fear. This may mean that she is 'Fearless' (the series title), but the books in which she appears provide fast-paced, often tense reading experiences as Gaia tackles gangs of armed youths on the streets and in the parks of New York City, is constantly observed and tested by secret agents (official and unofficial), and at any point in a text may have multiple assassins on her trail. She doesn't know about all of her enemies, but the reader does and so mistrusts her fearless state and reactions. It remains to be seen how Gaia's life will evolve, and whether the series will be as successful for Pascal and her publishers as Sweet Valley High.

Perhaps the two best-known examples of the new female protagonist of recent years are the very different characters of Scully, the highly cerebral, scientific, self-controlled agent of law and order in the X-Files and Buffy, the eponymous kick-boxing, intuitive, unorthodox would-be fashion-victim protagonist of Buffy the Vampire Slayer. Though neither the X-Files nor Buffy the Vampire Slayer originally appeared in book form or was aimed at a young audience, both have been packaged in a range of print forms, and both have been extremely popular with adolescent readers and viewers.

The way that the X-Files and Buffy have moved between audiences and media is typical of the construction and dissemination of narratives for young people at the beginning of the twenty-first century; perhaps especially in the domain of frightening fiction. Many of the most popular books and series today often either have their origins in screened (film and/or television) stories, or give birth to film/television/video versions. Another common feature is that texts originally created for one audience, usually adults, are appropriated and re-presented for young people. Each of these transformations is the product of commercial decisions based on the recognition of potential new markets. The practice is not new in juvenile publishing; in fact, most of the earliest books now associated with the juvenile canon were originally written for adults, among them Pilgrim's Progress, Robinson Crusoe, and Gulliver's Travels. However, the speed with which such transitions are now made, the many permutations they generate (the book of the film, the film of the book, the book of the film of the TV series, the 'Watcher's Guide', the 'Fact File', the comic, and so on), and the freedom with which texts are adapted for different audiences and formats affects both the core narrative and the 'reader's' response.

The potential for texts to mutate in the reader's mind after being encountered in different media, or indeed, when a new version of a text is offered in the same medium such as a remake of a film or a new production of a play is always present. However, the range of media through which a reader may encounter texts such as the *X-Files* or *Buffy* more or less simultaneously means that the process is more complex and potentially more capable of deliberate cross-media references on the part of writers than for, say, a new version of a Shakespeare play or a new adaptation of a Jane Austen novel. Added to writers' opportunities to move between narrative versions is the likelihood that readers will import ghostly versions of narratives encountered in one form while experiencing them in another. In the case of young viewers the whole process is intensified by discussing texts with peers, merchandising, and even fashion statements arising from or feeding into particular cult books, films and programmes. Since none of the texts being discussed in the main part of this study has undergone the full range of such transformations, it seems appropriate here to look in more detail at the phenomenon, using the *X-Files* and *Buffy the Vampire Slayer* as case studies. The two represent different but influential strands of frightening fiction, and by comparing them it is possible to explore the genre's impact on, and uses for young readers.

'The Truth is Out There ... ': The *X-Files*

In her controversial book, *Hystories: Hysterical Epidemics and Modern Culture*, Elaine Showalter argues that as Western culture moved towards the end of the twentieth century and the end of the second millennium, it became increasingly prone to what she calls 'epidemics of hysterical disorders' typified by Gulf War and Chronic Fatigue (ME) syndromes; accounts of alien abductions; anxiety about unidentified viruses, fluoridation of water; chemical warfare; anorexic and bulimic behaviour; tales of satanic ritual abuse; recovered memories of childhood sexual abuse; Multiple Personality Disorder, and the widespread conviction that hugely powerful governmental, economic and medical cartels deliberately withhold and manipulate information vital to the well-being and health of the population.

Showalter, a historian of medicine and psychoanalysis as well as a renowned feminist literary critic, argues that hysteria takes the form of and is spread by stories. Narratives predicated on the acceptance of unseen forces, conspiracies and cover-ups, she suggests, are manifestations of cultural hysteria and impede the ability of groups to function at emotional, social, and global levels. As the *X-Files* and their print-based offspring demonstrate, texts produced for and/or read by the young are not immune from this trend to embrace conspiracy theories and accusatory modes. If Showalter is even partially correct and if, as she insists, this propensity is spread through stories, then it behoves us to scrutinize the stories we are telling to young people, and to consider their effects. Could the popularity of some frightening fiction be a symptom – or even an agent – of the kind of epidemic she describes? Do some of these narratives have the potential to act as antidotes or prophylactics against it? Analyses of X-Files and Buffy texts suggest both effects are possible.

The central plot of X-Files narratives hangs on the assumption that all governments are duplicitous, power structures deliberately obscure, the media corrupt, and most people and relationships untrustworthy: precisely the kind of world view Showalter associates with new hysterical epidemics. Nothing is reliable, too much cannot (or will not) be explained. Moreover, the virtually unchecked flow of information now accessible through such things as instant media, computer databases and the Internet makes it possible to know about, document and disseminate events that might previously have been concealed or repressed for long periods, and fuels speculation about others, past and present, that may or may not have occurred. This is the paradox at the centre of the X-Files: though it is now possible to have more information than ever before and there is much talk of 'freedom of information' there is also a greater sense of what has been and is being withheld, repressed or concealed.

The contradictions inherent in this situation are precisely those that underlie many of the new hysterical epidemics discussed in Hystories, and the X-Files do seem to be a response to the conditions that generate new hysterias, including specific events and issues that have preoccupied British and American culture over recent decades. For instance, in X-Files narratives it is possible to find such things as residual Cold War anxieties about Communist infiltration, and fear of contamination by chemicals and by diseases, whether these are spawned accidentally or deliberately manufactured. Alien invasion, a powerful fear which frequently took narrative form in the early part of the last century, has in the X-Files been reinvigorated by suggestions of a suspect alliance between government, the scientific establishment and unknown aliens. For instance, many X-Files narratives recount Mulder and Scully's discoveries of top-secret government projects designed to interbreed humans and aliens.

X-Files narratives also seem to mimic the form of the 'stories' associated with new hysterias. To begin with, the various plot strands which make up X-Files narratives do not develop consistently or coherently; rather, they follow the shifting logic of nightmare. For instance, the parameters of the 'X-Files' themselves are undefined: it seems almost any strange or inconclusive event may be added to the files, and the reasons for secrecy, cover-up and denial are equally broad. Mulder and Scully's investigations include empirically sound tests and verifiable evidence, but also fugitive primary material, elusive witnesses, and conclusions arrived at as much through intuition and the recognition of patterns as by the careful accumulation and verification of facts associated with the FBI. The reader/viewer is left with the feeling that there *is* a case to be answered, but uncertain as to what it is, what it means, or who is responsible.

In this, *X-Files* texts are again typical of a new hysterical interpretation of the world, for as she describes them, the majority of Showalter's new hysterics shape their stories in accordance with a master plot suffused with the conviction that conspiracies are all around. This is a significant departure from traditional texts dealing in monsters, transgression, and the unknown, as Mandy Treagus observes in her analysis of 'Television Gothic: The *X-Files*':

> In some respects, not much has changed since *Frankenstein*. We are still trying to work out humanity, especially in the light of current challenges to the boundaries of what is human ... there has always been human fear and the search for meaning, and they have generally been linked in some kind of religious expression. That is not the case here ... [the *X-Files*] does not suggest that nobody knows what is going on and that there is no meaning. It suggests, rather, that somebody does know what is going on, but they are not telling.[18]

X-Files narratives display many of the attributes Showalter associates with late-twentieth century, postmodern forms of hysteria. On the spectrum of frightening fiction, they belong to the range closest to horror, as their narrative aim is to leave the reader or viewer feeling distinctly uneasy. Although they deal with many of the same anxieties, the narrative drive of *Buffy the Vampire Slayer* texts is fundamentally different.

Buffy: Icon and antidote
Buffy Ann Summers is the 'Chosen One': a girl born to slay the vampires and demons who threaten to overwhelm humankind. As she is introduced in the earliest film version of the text, Buffy is a high-school student, living in Sunnydale, California, which is situated over the mouth of Hell (the 'Hellmouth') and thus a hotbed of vampiric activity. Each Slayer has a Watcher, who fulfils the astonishingly diverse roles of scholar, mentor, personal trainer and intermediary (in

Buffy's case, with her school authorities in the form of Principal Skinner). Buffy's Watcher, Giles the school librarian, is a bizarre creation, as unlikely as Frankenstein's monster. Formerly the head of the British Library, he now runs the Sunnydale High library where he keeps an eclectic collection of tomes unlikely to be of any use to students trying to pass high-school English, French or Biology. Unusually for a Slayer, Buffy also has a small circle of friends who know who – and what – she is. Her best friend, Willow Rosenberg, is one of these as well as being a computer nerd who dates a werewolf rock musician.

Buffy texts in all their formats appeal to the same appetite for tales which combine the supernatural and the frightening which underpins the success of frightening fiction such as books in the Point Horror series. Unlike the *X-Files*, which offer a largely paranoid view of the world and so potentially feed new hysterical reactions, *Buffy* narratives are essentially optimistic and reassuring. If there are strains of frightening fiction capable of acting as antidotes to new hysteria, *Buffy* would seem to be one. A reason for this is that just as hysterics express their symptoms iconically – that is, they act out their symptoms through or on their own bodies – so *Buffy* texts work through iconic forms of communication. Through their setting, plot, and characters, they give expression to some of the areas of anxiety in Western culture associated with new hysterias. In Freudian analysis the treatment of hysteria involves patients learning to construct coherent narratives about their lives with the help of an analyst whose task is largely to help patients complete their stories: 'traumatic memories "need to be integrated into existing mental schemes, and be translated into narrative language," in order to be relived and relieved'.[19] Readers of the *Buffy* texts encounter a succession of already coherent accounts which reverse the dynamic of paranoia typical of narratives in the *X-Files* mode.

For some readers/viewers such texts may help to inscribe a sense of agency. Agency is proffered because, although as in the *X-Files* there *are* constant threats to civilization through mysterious, paranormal creatures and activities, and there *is* a need for constant vigilance as familiar people and places mutate, conspire and betray, ultimately in *Buffy* texts all enemies can be identified and overcome. Unlike the *X-Files* and its textual clones, which repeatedly assert that 'the truth is out there' but can never be conclusively attained or communicated, in *Buffy* stories there is a definitive body of knowledge. It is shared by Watchers and Slayers, who make use of all the technological, mass-media forms of communication implicated in the spread of hysterical epidemics. In fact, *Buffy* plots are driven from the position of insider knowledge which, though often incomplete or oracular, is never deliberately false.

The power dynamic which characterizes *Buffy* stories rings several interesting changes on frightening fiction dealing in hysteria in ways which are significant given its end-of-the-millennium popularity. Traditionally hysteria is the domain of the female and at times of cultural crisis or radical transition such as entering a new millennium, invites slavish adherence to identified leaders. Significantly, Buffy is not a leader, but a member of a team, each of whom has her/his own area of expertise, and in these texts hysteria is sex and gender blind. Hysteria is the hallmark of the vampires, both male and female, who swarm from the Hellmouth. Suspended between life and death they symbolize all those who have lost contact with the real world through such things as excessive self-indulgence, self-loathing, and total capitulation to consumption – usually of sex, drugs and fashion. They live in a constant state of abjection and disorientation, ever in search of new masters.

Many of Showalter's new hysterias are embodied and laid to rest in *Buffy* texts, foremost among them Recovered Memory Syndrome which, according to many therapists, dominates the mental health debate in North America and is becoming increasingly significant elsewhere.[20] Whether or not individuals believe in the 'memories' which surface through analysis and other forms of treatment, their consequences for families and individuals have frequently been devastating; usually because they feature incidents of childhood abuse. Because the phenomenon was relatively widespread during the late twentieth century and affected families from all walks of life, such 'memories' came to be an area of cultural as well as individual anxiety. Thinking again of *Buffy* books as a form of iconic communication, it is possible to read them as transforming the silent discourses of fear and repression into visual, coherent and manageable narratives. In such a reading, the vampires enact the drives and dynamics of abuse and its survivors. For instance, frequently *Buffy* plots revolve around love stories featuring ghostly suitors who return intent on reclaiming lovers or taking vengeance on those who rejected them in life.[21] Like victims of childhood abuse, the vampires live in a world of secrets: their vampirism itself is a condition which must be concealed, a secret that cannot be told. In a particularly interesting twist to this aspect of the stories, Buffy's own love life seems to exhibit the compulsion to repeat the dynamics of abuse in subsequent relationships. Although we know very little about her father (her parents are divorced and he doesn't feature in the texts), Buffy's first and only significant 'boyfriend', Angel, is a vampire. This means both that, since she is the Vampire Slayer and he is a vampire their love is forbidden/transgressive/taboo, *and* that he is more than old enough to be her father. Although he inhabits the body of a young man, Angel is 271 years older than Buffy!

The *Buffy* books seem to explore the anxieties around Recovered Memory Syndrome and new hysterias in many other ways too. For instance, Buffy moves in a world in which cannibalistic desires and satanic rituals are commonplace, and in her two personae (Buffy Summers, teenage fashion victim and the Slayer) she personifies the phenomenon of splitting out. Splitting out, in which one or more new personalities are formed in response to trauma, is often a defense mechanism associated with childhood abuse and capable of resulting in Multiple Personality Disorder which is, according to Showalter, another manifestation of new hysteria.

Working through the *Buffy* series it is possible to identify all the symptoms of paranoia and hysteria Showalter lists in *Hystories*. Significantly, as well as presenting the symptoms the texts vanquish them. They provide textual forums for acting out, completing, and so helping to dislodge areas of cultural anxiety. In this way they represent a form of frightening fiction which may be able to combat the miasma of hysteria and paranoia that can simultaneously paralyse and terrorize young people in contemporary society. Over the next three chapters of this study Geraldine Brennan and Kevin McCarron will explore the nature and possible effects of reading other forms of frightening fiction directed at young readers. While all of the texts work differently, none of them is boring. Being scared is a great incentive for turning pages . . . read on if you dare!

Notes

1 Figure supplied by Scholastic on 13/4/00.
2 M. Barker (1984) *A Haunt of Fears: The Strange History of the British Horror Comics Campaign*. London: Pluto Press, p. 5.
3 K. McCarron (1994) 'Point Horror and the Point of Horror', in A. Hogan (ed.), *Researching Children's Literature*. Southampton: LSU College of Higher Education, p. 28.
4 Sussex University, 14/4/00.
5 See, for example, T. Todorov's (1973) *The Fantastic: A Structural Approach to a Literary Genre* (trans. R. Howard). Cleveland and London: Press of Case Western Reserve University.
6 J. Grixti (1989) *Terrors of Uncertainty: The Cultural Contexts of Horror Fiction*. London: Routledge. Grixti, too, utilizes a broad definition of horror, which he sees as being primarily engaged in offering 'redescriptions of reality' (x) intended to propose 'the contemplation and evaluation of shared uncertainty' (xii).
7 *Ibid.*, p. viii.
8 Figures supplied by Scholastic on 13/4/00.

9 N. Auerbach (1995) *Our Vampires, Ourselves*. London: University of Chicago Press, p. 3.
10 J. Appleyard (1991) *Becoming a Reader: The Experience of Fiction from Childhood to Adulthood*. Cambridge: Cambridge University Press, p. 109.
11 *Ibid.*, p. 97.
12 R. Jackson (1981) *Fantasy: The Literature of Subversion*. London and New York: Routledge, pp. 70–86.
13 Vice, S. (ed.) (1997) *Beyond the Pleasure Dome: Writings and Addiction from the Romantics*. London: Futura, p. 163.
14 Jackson, *op. cit.*, p. 68.
15 C. Sarland (1991) *Young People Reading: Culture and Response*. Milton Keynes: Open University Press, p. 63.
16 K. Reynolds *et al.* (1996) *Young People's Reading at the End of the Century*. London: Book Trust, Question 35, p. 74.
17 Sarland, *op. cit.*, p. 54.
18 S. Hosking and D. Schwerdt (eds) (1999) *Extensions: Essays in English Studies from Shakespeare to the Spice Girls*. Adelaide: Wakefield Press, p. 197.
19 E. Showalter, quoting A. Van der Kolk Bessel in E. Showalter (1997) *Hystories: Hysterical Epidemics and Modern Culture*. London: Picador, p. 145.
20 See Crews and Webster in Showalter, *op. cit.*, p. 146.
21 I am paraphrasing Jan Marsh's analysis of Christina Rossetti's *Goblin Market* as quoted in Showalter, *op. cit.*, p. 90.

CHAPTER 1

Point Horror and the Point of Horror

Kevin McCarron

' *"Oh, you young people and your obsession with horror"* '.
Teacher's Pet, Richie Tankersley Cusick

> One of the most obvious features of horror is the way it retells the same stories decade after decade, sequel after sequel – stories that are often age-old and close to world-wide to begin with … it is perhaps at the subgeneric level (possession, slasher, vampire) that the 'yet again' nature of the enterprise is most evident, but in either case, it is surely fair to say that horror is probably the most convention-bound of all popular genres.
>
> *Men, Women, and Chainsaws*, Carol J. Clover

The Point Horror series is a cultural phenomenon. In an article in *The Observer*, Andrew Billen observes:

> Since Point Horror was launched in 1991, its 41 titles have sold some six million copies to British children. With a new Point Horror published every month, with audio tapes available, and with five imitator series from other publishers – Terror Academy, Horror High, The Power, Nightmares and Horoscopes – on the shelves, young readers, male and female, do not so much read this genre as mainline it.[1]

Point Horror Unleashed, discussed by Geraldine Brennan in the final part of this book, has recently joined this list. Given also that adolescent readers are in the habit of exchanging these horror novels, the numbers of texts actually read, as opposed to purchased, may well exceed ten million. The image of 'mainlining' used in the quotation above is characteristic of much of the discussion that has been generated by the Point Horror series, and by adolescent horror fiction overall. As Kim Reynolds observes in the Introduction, the discourse of dependency which typifies debates about fruit machines, video games, and anything else of which adults disapprove, permeates discussions about the popularity of horror fiction among the young. Part of the appeal of Point Horror fiction is obvious, and Billen refers to a crucial aspect of the novels' appeal in his article: 'They rarely run to more than 180 pages, but superficially look like another Stephen King blockbuster. Key to their success is that, although they are children's books, they do not look it.'[2] They are also undemanding in terms of vocabulary, written in short chapters, in short sentences, and in short paragraphs; indeed some of the paragraphs run to no more than a single line. However, success on the scale that Point Horror has achieved deserves a more searching scrutiny than listing the immediately obvious. Writing about the public response to the film *The Exorcist*, John Nicholson observes: 'Horror has always been a coded language.'[3] In the following chapter I want to consider some of the codes and conventions central to Point Horror novels and suggest that Point Horror novels have a value beyond that of satisfying a craving which they have themselves created.

The following quotations are all taken from novels in the Point Horror or Nightmare series, books which are clearly aimed at the adolescent audience:

> The great glittering blade hooked him under the chin. It caught, fractionally. Wrenched sideways, the boy dressed like Freddie was in shock long before it was finished. He never knew he was dead. (D. E. Athkins, *The Cemetery* (1993), p. 54)

> The back of Chip's head had been covered with blood, but the back of Ron's was missing, as though it had been blown away, leaving only a mass of bloody pulp. (Bebe Faas Rice, *Class Trip* (1993), p. 148)

> The man with the torch plunged a knife deep into Karen's heart, then pulled it out. She was barely alive as he threw her on top of the bodies of her brother and boyfriend ... The last sound that Karen heard before she died was that of police sirens ... (David Belbin, *The Buyers* (1992), p. 287)

It is often assumed that the genre's reliance on extreme violence and its depiction of graphically detailed deaths, such as those quoted above, are the primary reasons for its extraordinary, and pernicious, hold over the adolescent reader. This may indeed be the case, but it is also the case that adult readers of adolescent horror fiction have the status of 'guests' when reading. Peter Hunt notes of non-adult readers that they are far more competent text-handlers than is generally assumed, but, he stresses, 'even so, it is difficult to replicate their encounters with texts'.[4] Freud acknowledges much the same difficulty in fully apprehending the reading experience of another person when he writes in his influential essay on horror 'The Uncanny' that, 'it had been a long time since he had experienced or heard of anything which had given him an uncanny impression'.[5] In their role as guests, adult readers, invited or uninvited, open-minded or censorious, may not always realize what it is that is being celebrated, criticized, rejected, or endorsed in the texts they read.

Stephen King, the most successful horror writer in the genre's history, writes in his study of horror, *Danse Macabre*: 'Begin by assuming that the tale of horror, no matter how primitive, is allegorical by its very nature; that it is symbolic. Assume that it is talking to us, like a patient on a psychoanalyst's couch, about one thing while it means another.'[6] It is noticeable that critics of adolescent horror fiction rarely, if ever, accept that the primary concern of the genre is precisely what it appears to be – death and the fear of death. Noel Carroll suggests, for example, 'horror stories are predominantly concerned with knowledge as a theme'. For Carol Clover, horror's appeal lies in its 'engagement of repressed fears and desires and its re-enactment of the residual conflict surrounding those feelings'. James B. Twitchell writes:

> anthropologists, sociologists, and psychologists all agree: the primary concern of early adolescence is the transition from individual and isolated sexuality to pairing and reproductive sexuality. It is a concern fraught with unarticulated anxiety and thus ripe for the experience of horror.

For these writers, and numerous others, death in adolescent horror fiction is a mask, which, when removed, reveals that the texts' true concerns are sexual, epistemological, and social. However my contention is that when death's mask is removed, what lies behind it is death – and yet, paradoxically, the primary concern of such texts is to persuade the adolescent reader that death does not exist.

The black comedy of many of these texts is often overlooked by commentators, just as it is in appraisals of the *Nightmare on Elm Street* films, a series which, like much adolescent horror fiction, although far more disturbingly, breaks down the distinction between waking and sleeping and between the living and the dead. The darkly comic moments in Point Horror novels, as in the *Nightmare* films, contribute to the depiction of death as displaced, 'unreal'. A not-uncharacteristic episode in Richie Tankersley's Cusick's *Teacher's Pet* (1991) has Gideon asking Pearce if he has found William: 'For another long moment there was silence. "Parts of him," Pearce said at last' (127). A sly, intertextual humour is also a characteristic feature of many of the novels. In Cusick's *Trick or Treat* (1991), Martha, who is fond of Emily Dickinson's poetry, is taken to a Hallowe'en party by Blake in his car: 'Something hideous sat in the driver's seat and grinned at her fiendishly from the loose folds of a hooded cape ... "I'm Death," the thing said. And then it opened her door and beckoned. "Climb on in"' (179). Presumably this reference to Dickinson's famous lines 'Because I could not stop for Death/He kindly stopped for me' goes unrecognized by the majority of the novel's readers, but not by the protagonist. Death is never 'kind' in Point Horror novels, but it is never real either.

Several of the subsidiary characters in the novels are passionately fond of horror videos with wildly, comically, improbable names. In Nicholas Adams' *I.O.U* a character says enthusiastically of a video: '"This is a classic – *I Ate Your Guts*"' (59). It is noticeable that the biggest fans of such films are immediately suspected of whatever murder and mayhem is occurring around them – and are always innocent. In R. L. Stine's *The Baby-Sitter II* (1992) the child, Eli, gleefully watches a particularly brutal horror film, much to the alarm of Jenny, who is the eponymous babysitter: 'I don't want to turn this into a battle, Jenny thought, watching the man with the ax start chopping away at a teenage girl who looked a lot like Jenny' (51). Later, Eli's father responds to Jenny's concern by saying '"Well, maybe he'll get the blood and gore out of his system that way"' (58). Eli's father's defence of the genre is used, overtly and covertly, on numerous occasions throughout the Point Horror series, which consistently protects itself from claims that it corrupts or depraves its readers. The intertextual allusions, to 'real' texts and to comically imaginary ones, as well as the pervasive black humour, emphasize for the reader the 'unrealistic' nature of such novels, as well as the illusory status of depictions of death in adolescent horror fiction.

Adolescent horror narratives can be seen as 'tutor texts' – and the subject in which they offer the reader most 'tuition' is death. In *Dreadful Pleasures* Twitchell ignores the symbolic dimension of horror fiction when he writes: 'Essentially, horror ... has more to do with laying down the rules of socialization and extrapolating a hidden code of sexual behaviour' (66). Horror texts do indeed have a socializing function, and sexuality is a concern of such narratives, but their primary concern is with the initiation of the adolescent reader into the ways in which the subject of death is regarded and represented in our culture. The real horror in Point Horror is not murder, but death. Murder, like a fatal accident, is a subset of death – but, reassuringly, it is unnatural. Despite the myriad stabbings and clubbings and decapitations, despite the numbers of insidious whispers promising such fates, despite the dead tormenting the living with their refusal to acknowledge that they no longer exist, it is what is *absent* from adolescent horror fiction which reveals its essential function. There are no sick people, there are no old people, there are no natural deaths. There are no funerals; there are no cremations. There are no priests, vicars, or nuns. There are no churches or cathedrals. Nobody ever visits the dead. Even in the thrillers, which are inevitably more socially mimetic than the supernatural stories, there are no grandparents. No parent, friend of the family, relative, or neighbour is ever represented as being above the age of forty five. Nobody ever dies of a heart attack, or cancer, or, most strikingly, of old age. Nobody ever commits suicide. Nobody talks of the dead – except in terms of fear and loathing. None of the dead who do return are ever presented as anything but malevolent; there are no benign spirits or guides. The suburban world depicted in adolescent horror fiction is one of extreme affluence, of space and opportunity, of sophisticated technology which is taken totally for granted by all the characters, but it is also, simultaneously, a world so horrified at the inevitability of death that it refuses to mention it – death as part of the natural order is literally inconceivable. This is a world in which death has become abnormal. The world depicted in adolescent horror fiction is one of cartoon violence and death, one which actually removes the reality of death from the adolescent consciousness. Virtually all deaths in Point Horror novels are accidental, in the sense that they are never part of the natural order.

In R. L. Stine's *The Hitchhiker* (1993) James reflects on his move to Key West: 'He had moved there with his aunt when he was twelve. After the accident. After both of his parents had been smeared across the highway' (3). In Richie Tankersley Cusick's *April Fools* (1990) Cobbs tells Belinda how Adam's aunt and uncle died: ' "The car plunged down an embankment and caught fire. Adam's uncle was killed outright. His aunt died later that night in hospital"' (153). Although car crashes are the favoured form of accidental parental death, a variation occurs in Cusick's *The Lifeguard* (1993): ' "We were at the beach, and we'd gone out in the boat ... the boat turned over. Dad didn't make it. He saved my life ... but he drowned"' (173). In A.

Bates's *The Dead Game* (1989) we are given access to Jackson's thoughts on the subject of his father's death:

> He remembered when his father died. Jackson had been eight ...
> Industrial accident.
> Things had blurred. He'd seen death before – dead birds, cats, dogs. He'd seen mice caught in traps. But Dad?
> It didn't seem possible that someone so big, so good at shuffling cards and cooking stir-fry and cracking dumb jokes could be dead. It couldn't be real. (129)

The depiction of death as something that isn't 'real' is central to all these texts. Murder is also an accident, a breach of the natural order, and so in these novels death is always displaced from the realm of the 'real' and re-presented as the artificial – hence its attraction.

Parents, who are all too often dispatched in off-stage car crashes, perform other functions in their brief appearances. As Charles Sarland notes, in Point Horror, 'all the protagonists, except for Duffy in *The Fever* and Kate in *Teacher's Pet*, where it is not specified, come from single-parent families of one sort or another.'[7] In D. E. Athkins' *The Cemetery* (1993) Charity has a stepfather and in Caroline B. Cooney's *The Cheerleader* (1992) Althea's parents are never mentioned at all, while in Cooney's *Freeze Tag* (1993) and *The Perfume* (1993) Sinclair Smith's *Dream Date* (1993) and Diane Hoh's *The Accident* (1992) the protagonists have both parents but no siblings. However, even when protagonists do have both parents, the parents are invariably depicted as working – working themselves to death; certainly to the point of virtual invisibility.

Parental absence is never attributable to any activity other than work. In Diane Hoh's *The Fever* (1992) Duffy's mother apologizes for not being able visit her more often in hospital, where Duffy is convinced, correctly, that someone is trying to kill her: ' "But it's tax time, honey, and you know what that's like." ' Duffy's parents were accountants and she did know what tax time was like. She had picked a lousy time to get sick' (122). The very large majority of parents are upper middle class professionals, commuting long distances and working long hours, often in jobs they dislike. In *The Perfume* Cooney writes of Dove's father, who customarily eats four or five desserts a night: 'He had never liked his job, and it was a mystery to Dove why he stayed with it. It was a mystery to Father, too, and reaching for that line of desserts seemed to be linked with the eight grim hours of a job he loathed.' (27) Although Dove's mother, 'a busy accountant for a tax firm' loves her job, Dove thinks of her as she might an automaton:

'Dove thought that her mother's brain was filled with numbers instead of words, and that it clicked like an adding machine.' (26) In *The Dead Game* readers are told that Ming's parents: 'left the house before Ming got up. And like true bankers, got to work by six A.M ... ' (53). Often these busy professionals bring their work home with them and are depicted as defined solely by that work. In *I.O.U.* Sharon's father is described as putting down 'the legal papers he'd been looking at ... Being a lawyer, he was ready to argue his case with her ... '(29). Both Dove's mother and Sharon's father have died as people; they are machines for working. On the rare occasions that parents are not from the upper middle classes, they also work incessantly: ' "Mom's working double shifts at the hospital again. We never even see each other" ' (*April Fools*, (7)).

Working to the point of erasure is a form of death, but to work less is never envisaged; as for unemployment, like natural death, it is inconceivable. It is tempting to see the parents enslaved by a work ethic which the adolescent reader is being invited to criticize. However, work and death are linked in these novels. In Jackson's meditation on his father's fatal accident in *The Dead Game* he thinks: 'Grown-ups did strange things sometimes, muttering about taxes, IRS, parking tickets, stock markets.' (129–30) In this text, one of these adult concerns is connected to cars, the other three centre on money. Ming's parents are both bankers, while Dove's mother and both Duffy's parents are seen earning their living from taxation, the contribution the living pay to secure their comfort and safety. Death and taxes, as the saying goes, but the dead pay no taxes. When the dead have no value precisely because they can no longer contribute, then, logically, those seen as closest to death, the old and the sick, are afforded almost as little value, hence their absence from the novels. In adolescent horror fiction the old and the sick are effectively already dead, erased completely from the texts.

In *Criticism, Theory & Children's Literature* Peter Hunt notes that an awareness of language is 'the difference between saying what the book is about and what the book is *really* about' (68). I want to discuss what I think these Point Horror books are *really* about and by way of doing this to reply to Charles Sarland's article in *Signal*, quoted above. In his appraisal of ten Point Horror titles, Sarland offers his understanding of what the books are really about: 'Conflicts of friendship, loyalty and trust are familiar to us all, and Point Horror uses its thriller formulae to dramatize and play out just such conflicts' (54). This is true of the Point Horror 'thriller', but there are, in fact, two quite distinct Point Horror narratives, and Sarland only mentions one of them. In addition to the thriller there is also what can be called the 'juvenile novel of the supernatural'. Sarland read ten titles in the series: Richie Tankersley Cusick's *The Lifeguard* and *Teacher's Pet*, Carol Ellis's *My Secret Admirer*, Diane Hoh's *Funhouse*, *The Train* and *The Fever*, Sinclair Smith's *The Waitress* and R. L. Stine's *The Baby-Sitter*, *The Boyfriend* and *The Girlfriend*. He writes: 'All these are "psychological thrillers" ... In a sense "Point Horror" is something of a misnomer since none of the plots involves the supernatural or the metaphysical ... '(49). While this is quite true of the novels he refers to, it is simply not true of almost as many others which he does not mention, including Sinclair Smith's *Dream Date*, Diane Hoh's *The Accident*, R. L. Stine's *The Beach House* (1993), D. E. Athkins's *The Cemetery* and Caroline B. Cooney's *The Perfume*, *Freeze Tag*, *Night School* (1996), *The Cheerleader* (1992), *The Return of the Vampire* (1992), and *The Vampire's Promise* (1993). All of these novels feature some supernatural, always evil, phenomenon, and the implications of this narrative dualism are considerable for any appraisal of the Point Horror series.

Horror narratives in general, and Point Horror narratives in particular, are invariably structured around oppositions; the opposition between the real and the imaginary is a constant feature of these books. Structurally, the characteristic adolescent horror novel offers the reader a narrative in the course of which two opposing principles are conflated, generating unease, while the conclusion of the text reveals the separate nature of the opposing principles, restoring the reader's belief in the actual existence of duality. In *Dreadful Pleasures* Twitchell argues 'the fear that the youthful audience most want to exercise, or better yet, exorcise, is the fear most often resolved within the fairy-tale horror – the natural fear of separation and its consequences'.[8] However, only on the relatively superficial narrative level is separation, usually from one's peers, a process that excites unease in the adolescent reader; structurally, even ontologically, the recognition of separation, particularly between the living and the dead, is deeply reassuring. Athkins's *The Cemetery* elides the distinction between Life and Death, Cusick's *Teacher's Pet* denies the opposition between Writing and Life, Smith's *Dream Date* conflates the states of Waking and Dreaming, Cooney's *Freeze Tag* confuses Human with Mineral. However, in each case, and in numerous others, the apparent conflation is ultimately seen to be illusory and a reassuringly divisive perspective is returned to the adolescent universe. Adolescence itself, of course, can be viewed as a conceptual tool which bridges a number of traditional binary oppositions: innocence/knowledge, ignorance/ experience, infancy/maturity.

A crucial distinction which animates all the Point Horror novels is the one which exists between the sexes. In *Freeze Tag* Cooney writes: 'Brown stared at his fingernails, the way boys did, making fists and turning them up. Girls spread their fingers like fans and held them away' (138). This issue is central to both the thrillers and the supernatural stories: 'Only a guy could ask that question' (22), says Charity in *The Cemetery*, while in *The Cheerleader* Althea realizes: 'the real stamp of approval is from the girls ... Boys come and go, but girlfriends stay, and judge, and count' (86). Heterosexual romance is an absolute given in Point Horror, and the series consistently promotes a rigid, gendered separation. It is worth noting, though, that nobody ever has sex in a Point Horror novel. The promise of it, its imminence, however, is integral to the appeal of these novels for the adolescent reader. There are two uncomplicated sexes in Point Horror and no gay or lesbian characters. Again, however, I would suggest that this is not a moral issue. At the end of the thriller *Teacher's Pet* the villain, Pearce, whose name signals invasion, is discovered in a woman's clothes, and this gender confusion symbolizes an unacceptable level of chaos for this adolescent audience. Moments later the Poe-esque Rowena is revealed to be the scatterbrained but loveable Tawney, and, again, order is restored. Point Horror novels cannot tolerate disguise for too long. In Cooney's *The Perfume* Dove feels as though the mall itself is in disguise, as is suggested in this highly sophisticated image: 'A row of dark glass doors with dark metal edges stared at them like huge sunglasses over the mall's eyes' (70). That the world may actually not be as it appears is the source of real horror to Point Horror protagonists.

Stephen King writes in *Danse Macabre*: 'The melodies of the horror tale are simple and repetitive, and they are melodies of disestablishment and disintegration ... but another paradox is that the ritual outletting of these emotions seems to bring things back to a more stable and constructive state again.'[9] The restoration of order through the recognition of duality is the principal goal of all Point Horror narratives, thrillers and juvenile tales of the supernatural; in this they resemble detective novels, another genre often referred to as 'addictive', although not as much a cause for concern as Point Horror, probably because it is usually adults who are addicted. However, rather than seeing the Point Horror thrillers as 'Who Done Its', it might be more useful, given the way they unfold in a continuous present, to call them 'Who's Doing Its'. Sarland offers a concise summary of the plot of a typical Point Horror thriller:

The protagonists come under threat and discover that they don't know whom to trust. There will be a passage where they rehearse their relationship with each of the other characters, and each will come under suspicion. By the end of the story, after the killer has been identified and removed from the equation, interpersonal trust and social cohesiveness will be re-established. (51)

Again, an evaluation such as this stresses the social dimension of the texts, while I would suggest that the Point Horror thriller, like the Point Horror supernatural story, is primarily concerned with establishing differences and that, amongst other strategies, it uses the insider/outsider paradigm to do this. The existence of the group is reaffirmed by the assault upon it. To be able to isolate, then expel the Other means it can be recognized, that it does, after all, exist in some clearly perceptible manner exterior to the individuals who comprise the group. There are, to my knowledge, no novels in the series which manage to be both thrillers and tales of the supernatural, although several give the illusion of combining the two narrative modes. Diane Hoh's *The Train* (1993), for example, pretends to be about retribution from beyond the grave – but is not – while *The Cemetery* pretends to be a thriller about a psychopath who we assume will be known to the group, but is in actuality a supernatural story.

R. L. Stine

'If you can't believe in pizza, what can you believe in?'
The Baby-Sitter, R. L. Stine

Writing of horror fiction in general Clive Bloom notes: 'It has always been the critical mass of the genre that has been important rather than individual authors ... '[10]. This used to be true of adolescent horror fiction, and particularly of Point Horror; critics and readers alike spoke of the series, and if authors received a credit in discussions it was as much to do with convention and courtesy as with any notions of their individual and unique contributions. However, R. L. Stine has single-handedly changed everything. According to Andrew Billen:

There are not so very many multi-millionaire novelists. Even so, you are unlikely to have heard of R. L. Stine, one of the biggest earners of them all. Your children, however, if they are aged between 11 and 13, will know him as the author of *The Baby-Sitter*, *The Girlfriend*, *The Dead Girlfriend* and 12 other thrillers in the Point Horror series. Their younger brothers and sisters are likely to revere him too, for Stine has written 28 horror stories for

8 to 10 year olds under the brand name Goosebumps; in one heady week last autumn, his books took six out of the top eight places in the best sellers list for the age range. In his own gory way, he is the Enid Blyton *de nos jours*.[11]

By 1998, David Charter, in *The Times*, was able to write: 'An American horror writer tops the list of the most sought-after authors in the children's sections of Britain's libraries. R. L. Stine's spooky fare of walking scarecrows and reanimated mummies have made him a firm favourite with youngsters who have consigned the perennial favourite Roald Dahl to third place.'[12] Charter goes on to note 'Stine's phenomenal world-wide success, with sales of 180 million.'

One reason for Stine's extraordinary success may be that, unlike his Point Horror colleague Caroline B. Cooney, for example, Stine does not specialize in horror at all – his primary concern is with generating terror. Twitchell writes: 'the etiology of horror is *always* in dreams; while the basis of terror is in actuality. Thus, while the images may be similar, the interpretation of horror will finally be psychological, while the interpretation of terror will be contextual.'[13] The first of the R. L. Stine 'Special Editions' (1996) contains three of his best known novels: *The Baby-Sitter* (1989), *The Baby-Sitter II* (1991), and *The Baby-Sitter III* (1993). Before actually starting the first page of the first novel, the reader is promised three times 'A triple dose of Terror'. Unusually, perhaps, for a 'blurb', this one is accurate, and indeed the word 'terror', as opposed to 'horror', can be applied not only to virtually all of Stine's fiction, but to the great majority of all Point Horror novels. Terror is a rational phenomenon; horror, in essence, is an irrational, supernatural one. Stine has virtually no interest at all in the supernatural, although, as will be discussed, his use of images derived from the conventional stock of horror motifs, and his heavy reliance on the disturbed dreams of his protagonists give the illusion that he writes horror fiction. His plots are always rational, secular, and, ultimately, deeply reassuring to his adolescent audience. Stine has now written nearly one hundred novels. Obviously, a brief study such as this one cannot consider so many texts. I have, instead, selected a dozen of his best-known and most successful novels and will offer appraisals of these books, referring briefly to others in the course of the chapter.

The immensely successful 'Baby-Sitter trilogy' is characteristic of Stine's Point Horror fiction overall. All three of the novels constantly promise horror, but actually deliver a roller-coaster sequence of cliff-hangers, false scares, and red herrings, which culminate in an exciting, though thoroughly rational, expository final chapter. In *The Baby-Sitter*

Jenny babysits for Mr and Mrs Hagen every Tuesday and Thursday night. These nights become nightmarish, as she becomes convinced that somebody is trying to kill her. Her fears are exacerbated by the fact that several babysitters in the area have been attacked. One of Stine's favourite plot devices is to introduce a character who is fond of playing practical jokes, which permits a sequence of frightening cliff-hangers, which are revealed at the beginning of the succeeding chapter to be that character's idea of a joke. In Stine's *Hit and Run* (1992) this device accounts for the entire plot. In *The Baby-Sitter* Jenny's boyfriend, Chuck, plays a series of practical jokes on her as does the child, Donny. Eventually, however, her fears are proved well-founded when it is revealed that Mr Hagen himself has been terrifying her. He blames babysitters for the death of another of his children and has been pursuing a vendetta against them. Just as he is about to kill her, Detective Ferris, who has been watching the house, and whom Jenny had earlier thought was her persecutor, helps to save her life, and Mr Hagen falls over a cliff to his death.

Jenny is an archetypal Stine heroine. She is 16, an only child living with her mother, as her parents are divorced: 'A sudden flash of memory. She was a little girl, seven or eight. Her parents had just divorced. She was adjusting to the sudden emptiness, the strange feeling of life with one parent where a short while before, there had been two' (109). Jenny feels dowdy and inert compared to her best friend, Laura, who she believes is more attractive and so more confident, especially with boys. The novel is clearly concerned with evoking sensations of loneliness and inferiority, not untypical emotions for adolescents. Again, however, as is characteristic of much of Stine's writing, the novel is also intertextually playful. When Jenny first arrives at the house Donny is watching *Ghost Busters* on video, while later, trying to calm her nerves after one of Chuck's practical jokes, Jenny tries to read, only to find she has brought a Stephen King novel with her. These references to the world of the supernatural are in fact displaced by Stine's reliance on the actual, the rational. Amusingly, given Stine's reputation for gore, the lesson Jenny takes from her experiences is not dissimilar to the one Catherine Moorland takes from her adventures in Jane Austen's witty critique of the Gothic novel, *Northanger Abbey* (1816). On the concluding page of *The Baby-Sitter* Jenny says to Chuck '"I don't think I'll live in such a fantasy world anymore, letting my imagination run away with me all the time. The real world is interesting enough!"' (126).

The Baby-Sitter II is extremely well-plotted and is engaging throughout; doubtless the denouement has surprised many adult readers. The novel opens *in media res*, with Jenny re-telling the events of the previous novel to a psychiatrist, Dr Schindler. This is not only a shrewd device for updating the reader, it is integral to the plot, as this time Jenny's persecutor is eventually revealed to be the psychiatrist's receptionist, the splendidly, and symbolically, named Mrs Gurney. She was a former patient of Dr Schindler, is in love with him, and believes Jenny is a rival. Mrs Gurney, of course, has access to the transcripts of Jenny's sessions with Dr Schindler, and is able to tap into Jenny's deepest fears by pretending to be Mr Hagen, back from the dead, and seeking revenge.

The Baby-Sitter II offers several good examples of Stine's clever use of dreams continuously to imply a horrific, supernatural dimension to his fiction, which is invariably refuted by the rational explanations which conclude his novels:

> Mr Hagen grinned at her. One eye was missing, revealing a dry, empty socket. His skull showed through where pieces of his cheek and forehead flesh had decayed and fallen off ... A black bug crawled over his swollen tongue. He repeatedly licked his dry lips, but his tongue was dry was dry and caked with dirt.
>
> 'No!' Jenny screamed. 'Let me go! I'm *begging you*! You're dead! You're dead! You're dead! Let me go!'
>
> '*Jenny – I'm back!*' (191)

This scene concludes chapter 10. Chapter 11 opens: ' "Then I woke up, screaming my head off," Jenny said, twisting and untwisting a dark strand of hair. "Mom was already in my room, sitting on the edge of the bed, trying to wake me up, trying to get me out of that horrible dream" ' (192). Similarly, in the penultimate chapter of *The Baby-Sitter*, Jenny looks at Mr Hagen, who is preparing to kill her: 'He looked like one of those hideous undead monsters that stagger through the horror movies, eyes ablaze with fury, everything about them zombielike and dead' (120). The comparison between Mr Hagen and 'one of those hideous undead monsters' invokes the supernatural, just as the dreams do, without in any way compromising the mimetic mode of representation which is, ultimately, one of the principal reasons for Stine's success.

The Baby-Sitter III is every bit as clever. Unusually for Stine and the Point Horror series generally, most of the novel is set away from the suburbs, in the countryside, where Jenny has been sent to help her put the past behind her. *The Baby-Sitter III* offers a bifurcated narrative, with the perspective shifting between Jenny and her cousin, Debra. Rather robustly, for a Point Horror novel, Jenny actually goes mad, hence the shift to another character's perspective. In this novel, Jenny comes to believe she is Mr Hagen. She kidnaps the baby Debra is looking after, but, of course, no harm comes to the child. Madness, paradoxically a rational, explicable and human aberration, is decidedly preferable to a vengeful ghost. Indeed, Debra's reassuring comment to Jenny, before the latter's condition is known to her, or the reader, could actually serve as an epigraph to all of Stine's fiction: ' "People don't come back from the dead" ' (323). This is exactly what Stine's enormous adolescent audience want to be told.

While the 'Baby-Sitter trilogy' delivers rational explanations of ostensibly supernatural phenomena, the other characteristic Stine narrative promises no supernatural experiences but, instead, offers a narrative in which the protagonist becomes aware that she is being singled out for persecution of one kind or another. Of course neither the protagonist nor the reader knows the identity of her persecutor, who could be a stalker, a trickster, or even a murderer. Concomitantly, the protagonist is asked to choose romantically between two very different boys. Often the two plot lines converge, with one of the two boys revealed as the villain, or at least connected to the villain, while the other boy saves her. Those of Stine's novels which conform to this pattern may be rehearsing anxieties about the importance of making the correct love-choice, the need for which is beginning to be apprehended by the adolescent reader. The list of possible suspects who may be persecuting the protagonist steadily grows, raising issues of trust and loyalty. Then, as occurs in classic detective fiction, this list of suspects is reduced by the conversion of suspects into victims themselves. Eventually, of course, since all of Stine's novels seek closure, the villain is revealed. However, the villain in Stine's fiction is never revealed in the manner characteristic of the classic detective novel, where in the final chapter the detective calmly presents the evidence of her or his own ratiocinative powers to an assembled group of suspects, among whom will be the murderer. Stine usually has villains revealing themselves to the protagonist only in the act of physically trying to kill them.

Beach Party (1992) offers just such a sequence of persecution, a list of possible suspects, and two very different boys, both of whom the protagonist finds attractive:

She thought about Jerry, so good-looking, so sensitive, and caring ... so *nice*.

She stared at Vince, his short, spiky hair, the diamond stud in his ear, the bold, black tattoo on his hand.

How could she like two boys who were so totally different?
(134)

Billen writes of this choice Karen is being asked to make in his survey
of Point Horror for *The Observer*: 'no prizes for guessing which (*sic*) is
the psycho'.[14] The 'psycho' in *Beach Party* is Jerry, but Billen is unfair in
his implication that the villain is always the nice boy. This is far from
being the case, and it is surely to Stine's credit that he does not
invariably make the boy from the wrong side of the tracks the villain.
Karen's best friend, Ann-Marie, of course, becomes one of a long list of
people whom Karen suspects of terrorizing her, before being vindicated
by Jerry's disclosure that it has been he all along. As occurs in *The
Baby-Sitter*, Karen believes Ann-Marie is more attractive than she:
'Ann-Marie was as thin as ever. She looked like a fashion model with
her slight figure, her straight blonde hair cut fashionably short, her
emerald eyes, and her high cheekbones and pale, creamy skin' (2).
Distinctions, and dichotomies of these emphatic types animate all of
Stine's work. Difference, choice, and individual preference are the
concepts which are negotiated in the course of a substantial proportion
of Stine's Point Horror fiction. The terror experienced by Stine's
protagonists serves, primarily, to hasten their development, and so to
confirm their readiness for adult life by endorsing the correctness of
their judgements. In *Beach Party*, despite Ann-Marie's beauty, Karen
finds love with an extremely good-looking boy, who finds Karen more
attractive than Ann-Marie. A novel like *Beach Party*, typical of a
certain kind of Stine novel, is reassuring in many such ways: the villain
is real and not imaginary, the great majority of the protagonist's friends
can indeed be trusted, there is somebody to love for everybody, and
goodness triumphs over evil. Jerry, actually, is not evil but, a favourite
plot device in Stine's fiction, he has 'a split personality'. The
alternative self, which always manifests itself in anti-social activity, is
used to affirm the importance of an unambiguous and coherent unity.
The 'split personality' is a coded warning of the dangers inherent in not
maintaining a rigid sense of separation. In addition, the reliance on
madness as an explanation of apparently evil acts is, of course, also
deeply reassuring to the adolescent audience as it denies the existence
of pure malice. The protagonist is not being terrorized because
somebody does not like her, perhaps the real source of fear to an
adolescent girl, but because she has been unfortunate enough to
attract the attention of somebody who is no longer rational. In the
'Baby-Sitter trilogy' all three of the villains: Mr Hagen, Mrs Gurney,
and Jenny herself, are mad, at least as far as the Point Horror

readership is concerned.

Although it is rarely specified, the great majority of Point Horror narratives are set in contemporary, suburban America. *Beach Party* is set in Los Angeles, specifically in Venice Beach, but an exchange such as this, from Stine's *The Girlfriend* (1992), is as geographically precise as the series usually gets: ' "I wish you wouldn't say 'bogus' all the time," Lora said, squeezing his hand affectionately. "I mean, we're going to Princeton, you know, not Ohio State" ' (3). Moments later a subsidiary character says of a football team: ' "They beat Westerville 35 to zip and we could only tie Westerville" '(7). The reference to Westerville, a city which is just outside Columbus, the state capital of Ohio, suggests, at most, that the novel is set 'somewhere in Ohio'. The specifically American references are vitiated by this geographical vagueness, and readers are invited to see the values inscribed in the texts as universal. Lora is, of course, punished for her snobbery and it is observations of this kind which often lead those who analyse adolescent horror fiction to stress the moral dimensions of such texts.

The Girlfriend is unusual for a Stine novel in that the protagonist is male. In this novel, 17-year-old Scotty goes out, quite chastely, with another girl, Shannon, while his regular girlfriend, Lora, is out of town. Shannon begins to terrorize Scotty, trying to persuade him to drop Lora and go out with her. *The Girlfriend* is an adolescent *Fatal Attraction*. There is no sex and no death, at least no human deaths, as Shannon does murder Scotty's pet. Her behaviour becomes increasingly bizarre and violent until at the novel's conclusion she tries to kill him. It is at this point that a policeman, who has been following Shannon as a suspect, just as occurs in *The Baby-Sitter*, arrives to help and informs Scotty that Shannon is a murderer: ' "This one was sent up for manslaughter," Jarmusch said, holding tightly to Shannon's shoulders' (164). Shannon is, of course, mad. Jarmusch says to Scotty: ' "I've been trying to get enough hard evidence to show that she still needs help. I don't want her to do more time. I just want her to get the treatment she needs" ' (164). In the novel's final lines Lora suggests that perhaps she and Scotty are too young to be so settled, but this is only very tentatively raised. The morality of the novel is deeply conservative, and, throughout, *The Girlfriend* endorses caution, suppression, and stasis.

Beach House (1992) is a very unusual Stine novel. At the centre of the book is time travel. This occurrence is routine in Robert Westall's work, as will be seen, but it is a considerably more inexplicable phenomenon than is customarily represented within Stine's writing, or indeed within the Point Horror series overall. *Beach House* is also unusual structurally, in that it alternates between 'The Summer of 1956' and 'This Summer', the latter a clever device which maintains a continuous contemporaneity. Although it is unusual in its structure and in its use of time travel, *Beach House* is characteristic of Stine's fiction in its emphasis on dualism, not only in its setting in two different time periods. The first of the two protagonists, Maria, who is later stabbed by Buddy and eaten by sharks, is jealous of her friend Amy, who she thinks is more attractive. Again, two boys are placed in opposition to one another:

> Buddy was good-looking in a clean-cut sort of way, but shy and awkward. And sort of clumsy. He was intense, very serious, Maria realized ... And then there was Stuart ... Stuart was Mr Rock and Roll. Mr Real Cool Cat. Stuart was a lot of fun. Always joking, always messing around. Always snapping his fingers to some tune no one else could hear. Always combing his heavily Brylcreemed hair, which came up in tall wave in front and then was swept into a ducktail over his shirt collar in back. (6)

In *Beach House* it is again the 'nice' boy who is the murderer, although, true to form, it is made clear that Buddy is insane. Stine's intertextual allusions are tailored to the 'Summer of 1956', so that while in *The Baby-Sitter* Donny watches *Ghost Busters*, here the teenagers watch *The Creature from the Black Lagoon*. Virtually the whole of the novel is written in the realistic mode of representation, until the conclusion, set in the present, where it is revealed that Maria, from 1956, has travelled through time, using the beach house of the title, to avenge what happened to her and the death of her friends. However, there are flickers of the paranormal running throughout the novel. The first appearance of Buddy, for example, can, with hindsight, be seen as a mysterious event: '[Maria] had met Buddy her first day on the beach. He just popped up in the sand beside her, as if out of nowhere' (6). Later, as Maria walks along the beach, we read: 'What a crazy afternoon, Maria thought, smiling to herself. That Stuart is such a clown. And as she thought his name, he appeared beside her ... ' (14).

Such instances of what might be called 'magic' cleverly anticipate the non-realistic conclusion to the novel. Stine confines the very graphically depicted killings to 1956, perhaps thereby providing his characteristic reassurance, in this case that the past was more dangerous and violent than the present. It is also worth noting that the contemporary protagonist, Ashley, is less horrified by the brutal murders which Brad/Buddy has carried out than she is at the thought that her friends, Lucy and Kip, who have inadvertently gone back in time to 1956, are no longer as young as she is: 'Kip and Lucy are probably in their fifties by now. "How awful," Ashley muttered, shaking her head' (199–200).

That Kip and Lucy might be so old now provokes Ashley's compassion far more than their actual deaths would have done. I would suggest that one of the reasons Stine is so popular among adolescent readers is that this fearful episode is offered quite without irony.

Like *The Girlfriend*, *Hit and Run* (1992) is another of the numerous Stine novels in which nobody dies, or at least, in this case, nobody who was not dead prior to the commencement of the narrative. The promise of murder, like the promise of sex, is often quite sufficient for Stine's audience. As noted earlier, *Hit and Run* is a novel structured around a practical joke; this one happens to be repeated half a dozen times. In *Hit and Run*, a group of high school students, Eddie, Scott, Winks, and Cassie, run over a man while illegally driving Eddie's parents' car. Believing that they have killed him, they drive away without reporting the accident. Unfortunately for them the corpse keeps re-appearing all over town, threatening them all with revenge and death. The plot of *Hit and Run* is strikingly similar to that of Donna Tartt's *The Secret History*, also published in 1992. In *The Secret History*, a group of high-flying university students, intoxicated by a dangerous mixture of Nietzsche and Dionysus, kill a man in their car and drive away. In Tartt's novel the ensuing debate among the characters involved in the hit and run centres around rival understandings of concepts such as 'truth' and 'justice'. In *Hit and Run* the difference between right and wrong is, reasonably enough, not interrogated. What they did was 'wrong'; to tell the police would be 'right'. They are punished for their refusal to do the right thing by Eddie, who with the assistance of his cousin, Jerry, who conveniently works at the local morgue, has been terrifying them with a corpse which was already dead when they hit him. Eddie's explanation for his vindictive behaviour is that the group has always made fun of him. Group mockery is also the reason that Buddy slaughters everybody in sight in *Beach House*. The dubious moral system at work in Stine's fiction is clearly in evidence in such instances: it is wrong to make fun of somebody, not because it would cause them pain, but because they might cause you pain. Eddie is, of course, represented as mad: ' "Take it easy," Jerry insisted. "We're going to get you all the help you need, Eddie" ' (160).

Hit and Run is also typical of Stine's novels, and the Point Horror series in general, in its dismissive attitude to the old and the indigent.

When Eddie and Cassie visit Jerry in the morgue he plays a trick on them:

> 'So you guys want to see a corpse, huh?' Jerry asked. Without warning, he reached over to one of the wall lockers and pulled the handle.
>
> 'Jerry, stop!' Cassie pleaded.
>
> But she was too late. A wide drawer slid out. On it, only partially covered by a white sheet, was the nude body of an old man.
>
> 'Come on, man, put it away!' Eddie screamed.
>
> Jerry giggled.
>
> 'Yuck.' Cassie felt sick. The smell was overpowering.
>
> Jerry reached down to the dead man's feet. 'Tickle, tickle'. He tickled the sole of one foot. (119–20)

In one of the rarest episodes in the entire Point Horror series, the dead body of an old person, who has presumably died of natural causes, is actually seen by characters within a novel. The sight is repugnant, while Eddie's cry 'put it away' also hints at something obscene. Perhaps even more distastefully, the corpse which Eddie and Jerry use to play their vicious prank is clearly represented as deserving of no respect: ' "But – but who is he?" she demanded, glancing to the open car trunk. "Some homeless guy," Eddie replied, shrugging his narrow shoulders. "No one claimed him. So Jerry let me borrow him" ' (154).

The abuses and indignities to which the corpse is subjected are not queried by any of the other characters, who are simply relieved that he is not really a malevolent ghost who is haunting them. The novel actually concludes with the corpse being propped up against yet another front door – for one last joke.

Halloween Night (1993) is another Stine novel which contains only the continuous threat of death. Nobody dies, but the protagonist, Brenda, is terrorized throughout the novel and suspects all her friends, as well as her cousin, in turn. Eventually Dina is revealed as her persecutor. Dina's reason for her malicious behaviour is that Brenda provided insufficient support when her parents were divorcing. Dina is, of course, mad and, yet again, the villain is taken quietly away at the novel's conclusion to a place where she will receive assistance and, significantly, not punishment: ' "The police were very gentle and understanding with Dina," Halley said quietly, staring into her cup. "She'll get the help she needs," Brenda said' (184).

Divorce is central to the plot of *Halloween Night*, as for much of the novel the chief suspect is Brenda's cousin Halley, who is living at

Brenda's house until '"her stupid parents work out their stupid divorce"' (3). The ubiquity of divorce in Stine's novels, and in the Point Horror series overall, may well reflect a growing divorce rate and be designed to promote a sense of social realism in the novels. Conversely, however, the pervasiveness of divorce could serve an entirely different function, metaphorically representing an unspecified sense of alienation and loneliness for adolescent readers, even for those who have both parents.

Characteristically, *Halloween Night* shifts in and out of reality by utilizing dreams to promote the suggestion of the supernatural while remaining committed to mimetic realism:

> And then, as the hideous, jagged lips continued to move, the wet sucking sound growing louder, Brenda heard the jack-o'-lantern's voice, dry as wind, dry as death. The grin widened. The yellow eyes whirled. The mouth opened and closed.
>
> And the jack-o'-lantern rasped: 'SEE YOU ON HALLOW-EEN.' (71)

In virtually every one of Stine's novels, such an episode could *only* happen in a dream. Nevertheless, such incidents are frightening and their ontological status, in all likelihood, irrelevant to the adolescent's reading experience.

The Dead Girlfriend (1993) is unusual for Stine, as it is told in the first person. The narrator is Annie, a 16-year-old girl who has just moved with her family to a new town. Immediately upon arrival she meets Jonathan, who is good-looking and moody, quite irresistible. Jonathan's previous girlfriend, the gorgeous Louisa, died in mysterious circumstances, and sooner rather than later Annie is fearful for her own life as somebody begins to persecute her. The novel delivers deaths, rather than merely promising them and, as usual, there is a long list of suspects. Again, the plot borrows from *Fatal Attraction* when Annie's cat, Goggles, is boiled alive in a saucepan in the family kitchen. In *The Dead Girlfriend* Dawn is the killer, and she is clearly insane, demanding as she is led away at the novel's conclusion to be thrown off the cliffs to her death: 'When I turned back, both policemen were leading Dawn to their car. She was still struggling. Still screaming hysterically, "Throw me over! Throw me over, too!"' (181).

It is quite possible that in novels like *The Dead Girlfriend*, in which a central character is persecuted by an unknown character for unknown reasons, it is not the nature of the outrages committed throughout the novel which terrifies and so appeals to the adolescent reader, but rather it stems from the sense of being singled out for persecution.

Such a response, which exaggerates and dramatizes the importance of the protagonist/victim, is a form of narcissism, and perhaps deeply appealing to adolescent readers, who are beginning to realize that there may be nothing special about them at all. The sense of being at the centre of the universe remains at the novel's conclusion, while the terror ceases with the death or arrest of the perpetrator. The appeal here is to regressive and atavistic impulses in the reader and perhaps only the ratification of a besieged narcissism can explain the extraordinarily strong appeal of this type of predictable formula fiction.

The Witness (1994) is very neatly plotted and, like *The Baby-Sitter III* and The *Hitcher* in which it is the girls who are revealed as killers, has almost certainly surprised many adult readers. In most other respects, however, it is typical of Stine's Point Horror fiction. The female protagonist, Roxie, is terrorized throughout the novel for being 'the witness' of the title and, once more, the plot borrows from *Fatal Attraction*. In this case it is a pet turtle which is gruesomely murdered: 'The turtle sprawled lifelessly on the concrete. Its head had been smashed flat. Its shell was cracked in a dozen places' (129). Typically, Roxie must choose romantically between two boys, one of whom will prove that he loves her while the other will be revealed as the one who has been terrorizing her: 'Lee was really great-looking, Roxie thought, in a sullen, moody kind of way ... Terry, she realized, was sort of the opposite of Lee. He was big and funny and loud' (15). In *The Witness* it is the good-looking, moody boy who is Roxie's persecutor, and he is, of course, insane. *The Witness* builds up suspense not just through the cliff-hanging nature and structure of the episodes, but also through a sequence of direct omniscient observations by the narrator: 'It seemed like a simple bet. A fun bet between best friends. Who would ever believe it would lead Roxie to a horrifying murder?' (29). *The Witness*, as indeed its title implies, at least with hindsight, is much preoccupied with judicial issues. Roxie's father is a very busy lawyer, typically immersed in his work throughout the novel. His friendship with the local police dramatizes for Roxie the paradoxes and complexities of the legal process. Her father, for example, points out that a person cannot be arrested without proof, while the police indicate that they are unable to look for proof until somebody has been arrested. Between them, the lawyer and the police dramatize the dangers of relying on any organized judicial system when threatened with personal danger. Stine uses the sense of fear to accelerate the development of his characters and to dramatize the vital importance of making the correct choice. In her introduction to this book, Kim Reynolds writes of the *Buffy the Vampire Slayer* series that it is possible to identify within it all the symptoms of paranoia and hysteria which Elaine Showalter lists in her book *Hystories*. She goes on to suggest: 'They provide textual forums for acting out, completing, and so helping to dislodge areas of cultural anxiety. In this way they function as antidotes to the forms of hysteria and paranoia that can simultaneously paralyse and terrorize young people in contemporary society.' The emphatic link between the correct romantic choice and life, or the incorrect romantic choice and death, which is such a striking feature of so many of Stine's Point Horror novels, may well suggest that such texts are actually displacement sites for dramatizing anxieties about Aids.

Call Waiting (1994) is, again, preoccupied with issues of trust. The protagonist, Karen, starts receiving sinister and anonymous phone calls. The list of suspects includes her brother, Chris, her boyfriend, Ethan, her cousin, Adam, and her best friend, Micah. The reader is unlikely to suspect Karen herself, but it is indeed Karen who for the first half of the novel invents the calls to gain the sympathy of Ethan, who she fears is losing interest in her. *Call Waiting* is a 'cry wolf' narrative; when the calls start for real, nobody will believe that she is not still making them up herself. It is Micah who, interestingly, is not depicted as mad, who has been making the calls, hoping that Ethan will leave Karen for her. Such Machiavellian malice is clearly seen as the behaviour of a sane person, who simply wants a particular boy more than she wants a best friend. *Call Waiting* is a virtual compendium of many of Stine's favourite characters and situations. Karen's own bizarre behaviour, and her desperate need for Ethan, may be explained, not simply by her parents' divorce, which is a routine occurrence in Point Horror fiction, but by the emphatically stressed brutality of it: 'Before Ethan, Karen had spent a lot of lonely time. Her parents had had an angry divorce three years before. Karen's father had left home without even saying good-bye to her' (12). Karen's mother is forced to work long hours, linking her with dozens of parents in Stine's Point Horror fiction who rarely see their children. Karen's cousin, Adam, is one of those Stine characters whose interest in horror films makes them an immediate suspect, but who never commit an anti-social act. As I suggested earlier, such characters, and there are many of them throughout Stine's Point Horror fiction, serve as red herrings within individual novels, but they also serve self-reflexively to promote the essential innocence of the genre.

Karen's brother, Chris, is also a stock Stine type. He is a practical joker, which allows Stine to conclude many chapters with the promise of real terror: 'From out of the deep shadows, the boy's lifeless eyes stared up at Karen' (9). The 'boy' is actually a mannequin, placed in the car by her brother as a joke. Stine invariably prefers effect to truth in such instances. At the end of the novel, when Karen and Micah are physically fighting, Stine concludes a chapter by writing: 'And she shoved the burning hot poker through Karen's heart' (162). This is not at all what happens, which is that 'A hot cinder had leapt from the fire and burned through her sweater' (163). Much of Stine's work is a textual roller-coaster of suspense, fear, and terror, punctuated by moments of release from tension, and culminating in relief and satiation.

Stine's best-known detractor is the American commentator Diane West and Stine's views of her criticisms can be found in an interview conducted by Andrew Billen for *The Observer* in 1996:

> 'There is a woman in the US named Diane West who makes her living by attacking me. She writes articles and goes on television shows.'
> 'What's her beef?'
> 'She has this over-the-top theory comparing these books to pornography, in that they create the same sort of tingle for kids, the same sort of physical reaction.'
> 'Is there any evidence they cause infantile erections?'
> 'No one has ever mentioned it to me.'[15]

The disingenuousness, and gender specificity, of Billen's final query notwithstanding, it is difficult not to be cautiously in agreement with West. Much of Stine's Point Horror writing can be read as an extended 'tease', in which it is the physical response of the reader which is of paramount importance. Such an understanding of Stine's fiction can indeed link it with pornography, which is also to a large extent the 'art' of rendition or performance. The horror audience, like the pornography audience, is sufficiently competent in evaluating their specific texts to recognize that the formulaic plots and one-dimensional characterization are not grounds for criticism, but rather the necessary backdrops to the main attraction.

Caroline B. Cooney

> 'You cannot lose me,' said the instructor. 'You made a choice.'
> Choice.
>
> *Night School*, Caroline B. Cooney

In an article focusing on the displacement of traditional romance fiction in favour of horror fiction in Britain's libraries, Olga Craig wrote in *The Sunday Times*:

> R. L. Stine, [Point Horror's] top ghoul writer and author of *The Dead Girlfriend*, has soared from 155th to 27th in the top 200, joined by stablemate Caroline B. Cooney, author of *The Return of the Vampire*, who enters the top 200 for the first time with loans of more than 300,000.[16]

Craig's summary of Stine as a 'ghoul' writer is inaccurate, but can be applied to Caroline B. Cooney. While Stine is Point Horror's most successful writer of thrillers, Cooney is Point Horror's most successful writer of juvenile tales of the supernatural. Stine writes thrillers, but the Point Horror supernatural novels perform a series of different functions to the thrillers. The distinction between the thriller and the supernatural novels in the Point Horror series may well be gendered, in that the thrillers, which seek the appearance of realism, and always offer closure, can be seen as masculine, while the supernatural novels, particularly Cooney's, reject the realist mode of representation, and often resist closure.

The thrillers describe more actual deaths more violently than the supernatural tales, which displace the act of killing, privileged in the thriller, into an interest in the already dead, often depicting visits from the dead, or, connectedly, stressing the illusory nature of death. It is a crucial difference, one which can be seen to operate structurally. For instance, Sarland writes: 'I am arguing that the form of these thrillers dramatizes a plot about relationships, trust and friendship, along an insider/outsider paradigm.'[17] This is certainly the case as regards the thrillers, but the supernatural novels are structured differently, with the insider/outsider paradigm still being invoked, but often realized within one individual. Sarland stresses the social dimensions of the thrillers, arguing that they have value because they use the insider/outsider paradigm to construct narratives which interrogate worthwhile concepts such as trust and friendship.

However, in the supernatural novels the central opposition is the one that is perceived to exist between the living and the dead. Sarland's reading of the thrillers presupposes that the reader is most responsive to the thematic dimension of the text but it is as likely that the adolescent's pleasure, particularly in the supernatural stories, comes from the recognition of clearly defined oppositions, and not from any morality grafted on to the dichotomy. Both the thriller and the supernatural story do have one feature in common, and this feature is the cause of their immense popularity among adolescents: they celebrate the existence, the ontological reality, of distinctions.

The Point Horror supernatural story ultimately does what the Point

Horror thriller also does; it reaffirms the existence of duality, it restores a monological perspective to the adolescent universe, the supernatural story, perhaps aptly, assumes more forms than the thriller. Like Tolstoy's happy families, all the Point Horror thrillers are, ultimately, the same thriller, just as Sarland's summary of a typical thriller plot suggests. However, the Point Horror supernatural novels can be further subdivided. In *Danse Macabre* King writes of Bram Stoker's *Dracula* (1897), Robert Louis Stevenson's *Dr Jekyll and Mr Hyde* (1886) and Mary Shelley's *Frankenstein* (1816):

> at the centre of each stands (or slouches) a monster that has come to join and enlarge what Burt Hatlen calls the 'myth pool' – that body of fictive literature in which all of us, even the non-readers and those who do not go to the films, have communally bathed. Like an almost perfect Tarot hand representing our lusher concepts of evil, they can be neatly laid out: the Vampire, the Werewolf, and The Thing Without a Name.[18]

Throughout numerous Point Horror novels, Cooney presents variations on all three of these 'lusher concepts of evil'.

The villain of *Freeze Tag* (1993) is Lannie, a manifestation of The Thing With No Name, who is capable of freezing into total immobility, with a touch of her hand, anybody who displeases her. This includes Meghan, whose boyfriend, West, Lannie desires for herself. *Freeze Tag* is preoccupied with concepts such as order, control and regulation. When Lannie joins Meghan and West one afternoon, for example, we read: 'Meghan could not believe it. There were certain rules of etiquette and one was that you did not join a couple who were linked body and soul' (27). In an adolescent universe rules are comforting, not for their specific information value, as Sarland and Twitchell argue, but for establishing the sense of demarcation so reassuring to the adolescent reader. Lannie's crimes include her social transgressions, her inability to recognize adolescent regulations, quite as much as her tendency to turn her peers into ice cubes. In *Freeze Tag* nobody is really hurt and everybody learns a lesson in the desirability of comfort and order. The novel's preoccupation with order operates on a number of levels:

> There were to be raffles and games and prizes. There was a DJ (nobody wanted a band, they never played the songs right) and the chaperones were somebody else's parents. That was key. A good dance never had your own parents there. There was even a

dress code this time: dresses for girls and a shirt tucked in with a
tie for boys. (75)

What is of particular interest here is not simply the adolescents' desire
for a dress code, but the revealing parenthetical aside 'nobody wanted a
band; they never played the songs right', which can only mean 'not as
they sound on record'. There is no room here for the unpredictable,
the unexpected, the disorderly, all of which plunge the characters into
states of fear. The central irony of *Freeze Tag* is that Lannie's victims,
frozen in a state of death-like immobility, are only suffering, in an
accelerated manner, the eventual and desired fate of all the characters
in the novel. In several Point Horror novels the young characters
acknowledge their desire for routine and predictability. In A. Bates's
The Dead Game Ming says: ' "I like boring, peaceful days and nights. I
like things to be predictable" ' (117). In Cusick's *April Fools* Hilly says:
' "I've decided I really want my life dull and boring" ' (212). Lannie, in
The Dead Game, says to her friends: ' "Death ... It's the perfect
solution" ' (6). In these novels, the safety and comfort of death is often
offered as the perfect solution to the troublesome anarchy of life.

The desire for order in *Freeze Tag* can be seen in a comment such as
this: 'Tuesday and Brown felt weird thinking about their own brother
with their own best friend Meghan' (79). The second 'own' here makes
it clear that the feeling of 'weirdness' experienced by the children is an
unease generated by an inarticulate fear of incest, a concern also
recognized by Sarland in his survey of the Point Horror thrillers[19], and
as all Freudians are aware, the incest taboo enforces the boundary
between order and chaos. Sarland refers to his own book *Young People
Reading: Culture and Response* (1991) to note that, 'definition of
cultural boundaries is an important issue for young people' (60).
Although clearly true, the supernatural Point Horror novels also
emphasize for the reader that there are other boundaries, ontological
and epistemological, the definitions of which may be even more
important to them.

The second of King's categories is clearly applicable to Cooney's
'Vampire trilogy': *The Cheerleader* (1991), *The Return of the Vampire*
(1992), and *The Vampire's Promise* (1993). The very presence of a
vampire endorses one of Freud's comments on 'the uncanny': 'an
uncanny effect is often and easily produced when the distinction
between imagination and reality is effaced, as when something that we
have hitherto regarded as imaginary appears before us in reality ... '[20].
In addition, the fact that there are three of the novels endorses Freud's
observation that repetition is frequently a vital aspect of the uncanny

which often manifests itself as 'the constant recurrence of the same thing – the repetition of the same features or character-traits or vicissitudes, of the same crimes, or even the same names through several generations'.[21] In *The Cheerleader* a vampire promises Althea (the exotic names are a feature of the trilogy, and indeed very common in all Point Horror novels) popularity, the holy grail of conventional teenagers, but it must be at the expense of her peers, and Althea must give the vampire permission to feed off them. As she flourishes, they wither. Eventually, Althea refuses to sacrifice anybody else and accepts her lack of popularity before moving away.

In *The Return of the Vampire* Devnee's family move into the empty house and Devnee makes a similar bargain with the vampire, but she wishes for beauty and intelligence, recognizing that these qualities, and in that order, are the qualities that bestow popularity. As Devnee becomes beautiful, the luckless Aryssa loses her beauty. Similarly, after several visits from the vampire, the once intelligent Victoria becomes increasingly stupid while Devnee becomes increasingly brilliant. As occurs in *The Cheerleader* Devnee eventually refuses to sacrifice any more of her friends and the vampire is routed by her selflessness. She, too, moves away.

In *The Vampire's Promise* Cooney shifts her attention on to a group of teenagers (although within this group another young girl, Lacey, is the narrative's central focus) who become trapped in the now abandoned house by the vampire. He offers to let them go – if they will choose which one of them is to be his victim. As is characteristic of much horror fiction in general, Cooney refuses to close her vampire books; another novel is implicit in the conclusion of *The Vampire's Promise*:

> And the shadows that were the vampires hung in the sky, and departed, desperate, for they had only a few hours until dawn, only a few hours in which to find another nest.
> But usually, for vampires, a few hours is enough. (166)

Freud notes: 'The German word *unheimlich* [uncanny] is obviously the opposite of *heimlich* [homely] ... '[22] .The same house is central to Cooney's trilogy and it is possible to argue that another reason for the immense popularity of these particular novels is her conflation of two well-established horror conventions: the Haunted House and The Vampire. In *Danse Macabre* King quotes from Anne Rivers Siddons, the author of *The House Next Door* (1978), one of the most celebrated horror novels of the post-war years:

> The haunted house has always spoken specially and directly to
> me as the emblem of a particular horror. Maybe it's because, to a
> woman, her house is so much more than that: it is kingdom,
> responsibility, comfort, total world to her ... [23]

The central character in each of the three Vampire novels is, of course,
female.

Freud notes that a prominent characteristic of the uncanny is 'what
we should call telepathy – so that the one possesses knowledge, feelings
and experience in common with the other'.[24] This phenomenon occurs
in all three of the Vampire novels, as well as in *Twins* and *The Perfume*.
In *The Cheerleader* Althea only has to think of the vampire and he
appears: ' "You wanted me?" ' he said, "How flattering" ' (40). In *The
Return of the Vampire* the relationship between Devnee and the
vampire is even more intimate: ' "If it isn't worth it to you, I'll give it to
somebody else," said the vampire, from right inside her mind. She had
forgotten that he shared it with her now. That he could live there if he
chose' (86). In *The Vampire's Promise* the vampire reads the individual
minds of the whole group, mocking them and preventing them from
leaving.

Ultimately, in all three of the vampire novels, it is the conscience of
the central character which defeats the vampire; in each case the protagonist refuses to sacrifice more of her friends and accepts the
'ordinariness' which she has briefly transcended. Freud sees the
conscience as related to the issue of the *doppelgänger*, or double:

> The fact that an agency of this kind exists, which is able to treat
> the rest of the ego like an object – the fact, that is, that man is
> capable of self-observation – renders it possible to invest the old
> idea of a 'double' with a new meaning and to ascribe a number of
> things to it – above all, those things that seem to self-criticism to
> belong to the old surmounted narcissism of earliest times.[25]

It is possible to argue that the character's plight in each case reinforces,
or revivifies, the adolescent reader's own narcissistic impulses; impulses
they are being asked to abandon in order to participate fully in adult
life. The 'double' is, of course, a central issue in *The Perfume* and
Twins; the real issue being addressed in all these books is narcissism,
and the necessity of leaving it behind in childhood.

Freud further notes that the uncanny experience often contains a
'doubling, dividing, and interchanging of the self.'[26] This, too, is a
central feature of all three vampire novels, naturally enough, in that
the vampire effectively 'transplants' the desirable qualities of other

people into the protagonist, making it eventually difficult for her to determine exactly who she is. This issue is particularly striking in *The Return of the Vampire*, when Devnee wonders: 'Where is Aryssa? Is she me? Is she half me? Am I half her?' (77). Narratives which feature the 'double' in any of its forms can be seen as also raising questions which are in essence ontological; concerned with existence and identity.

Freud concludes his essay with an evaluation of the uncanny as manifested in literature, and notes, in a sentence which encapsulates many of the central concerns of the 'Vampire trilogy': 'let us take the uncanny associated with the omnipotence of thoughts, with the prompt fulfillment of wishes, with secret injurious powers and with the return of the dead.'[27] Immediate wish fulfilment is central to both *The Cheerleader* and *The Return of the Vampire*, in that both Althea and Devnee actively wish to be desirable. In the latter novel, Devnee makes her wish, in the full knowledge that it will harm Alyssa: 'She tried not to complete the wish. She tried to be satisfied with her lot in life. She failed. *Wish I were beautiful* (22).

Such wish fulfillment, an example of what Freud calls 'the omnipotence of thought' is primarily regressive and, therefore, immensely pleasurable to the adolescent who is only just beginning to realize that his or her own wishes will not be fulfilled immediately by a benign universe. In many of Cooney's supernatural novels wishes do come true, but then the conscience, the Freudian 'double', asserts its dominance. In this way, the books gratify and indulge adolescent narcissism, and yet, eventually, they also lead the adolescent forward, stressing the importance of adopting the role of a responsible adult, one who knows that the universe cannot be forced to obey the individual but that, rather, the individual must learn to come to terms with the world.

The 'Vampire trilogy' is sturdy in its morality, and yet offers a compliant understanding of sociability and popularity; all three novels have a rigid sense of either/or, as can be seen, for example, when Althea muses on popularity while she is sitting in the cafeteria: 'Cheerleaders, thought Althea, important people, jocks, the party crowd – they're always on another side of the room, sitting at a different table, laughing at a different joke. There's no way to cross that dividing line. Either you're popular or you aren't' (9). It is characteristic of Point Horror novels that there is no interrogation of the morality of this division – it is there, and everybody in the novels wants to be on the other side of the room: the smart, successful, sexy side. Unease in these novels has little to do with the social order, which is always perfectly acceptable as long as it is clearly defined. That is all adolescents want in these novels; not truth, not justice, but clarity. The most horrifying aspect of the vampire in *The Cheerleader* is not his immorality, which is taken for granted, but his ambivalent mortality and bodily status: 'He was half in the hemlocks. Indeed, he seemed half hemlock. His arms were among the needled branches; his hair might have been growing straight from the trees' (40). Neither one thing nor the other, the vampire's physicality exceeds boundaries; he is in a constant state of flux and cannot even be described as either dead or alive – he is both, simultaneously. The vampire's refusal to be contained and defined exemplifies the chaos and anarchy of things falling apart, the centre refusing to hold. It is this horror which must be overcome in the course of the narratives.

Cooney's *Night School* (1995) is a supernatural novel in which a group of four confused and alienated high school students attend an evening class during which they become disembodied and ghost-like: 'The world shifted under their feet ... They were shifted through the fault lines of the universe' (53). In order to get credit for the class from their instructor, who reeks of sewage and evil, they must nominate somebody weak whom the group will terrorize. The connections drawn throughout the novel between class credit and peer approval are impressively maintained. The plot is the same one as is used in the 'Vampire trilogy': characters are able to gratify their desires only by inflicting suffering on others. The moral is also the same: individual characters must not purchase peer approval at the expense of another person. Structurally, *Night School* is similar to *The Vampire's Promise* in that rather than focusing on an individual the point of view shifts across a group of characters. The deep fear that drives all four of the central characters is the fear of loneliness and, initially, each one of them is prepared to do anything to avoid that fate. When Mariah looks at the ineffectual and lonely substitute teacher, who will later be driven to a nervous breakdown by the group, Cooney writes: 'Mariah shuddered. What fate on earth was worse than being that lonely?' (43). However, the novel makes it clear that there are indeed worse fates than being that lonely. In addition, just as individual self-aggrandize-ment must be resisted, so too must the substitution of fantasy for reality. At the novel's conclusion Mariah realizes this: 'I pretend too much, she thought. I'm giving it up. Daydreams have their place, but not that much of a place. No more secret lives' (180). The distinction between reality and fantasy is emphatic.

The horror of a lack of definition is also central to the third of King's categories: the Werewolf. Cooney's *The Perfume* and *Twins* as well as Diane Hoh's *The Accident* belong in this category because, like *Dr Jekyll and Mr Hyde*, they are concerned with the transformation of one person into two very distinct 'selves': one of whom is good while the other is evil. In *The Perfume* Dove is 'taken over by', 'becomes', her evil sister Wing, who emerges when Dove buys the perfume of the title. The novel even self-reflexively refers to Stevenson's book when the psychiatrist says to Dove's parents: ' "*Dr Jekyll and Mr Hyde* as a story is boring. I cannot say the story has withstood the test of time" ' (138). He is forced, incidentally, to diagnose Dove as schizophrenic. *The Perfume* is, even for a Point Horror novel, unusually preoccupied with issues of identity and difference. Early in the novel we read: 'Dove could not bear things that matched. Identical objects seemed to accuse her of some crime, because she could not distinguish between them' (7). Later Dove's room is described: 'Nothing in Dove's room matched. Nothing was even. Nothing came in pairs. Nothing was folded with square corners. Identical things were impossible to endure' (17). The inside of the entire house stresses the horror created by the denial of boundaries: 'Balcony three was carpeted in the nubbly gray that waffled up the stairs and balconies, and here at the top it could not stop itself, but even covered the walls, forming little steplike seats' (17). Here, too, one thing blends into another, distinctions are not recognized; always a source of deepest unease to Point Horror protagonists, and, I would suggest, to adolescent readers of the novels as well.

Twins (1994) tells the story of Mary Lee and Madrigal, identical twins so uncannily similar that their parents decide to separate them by sending Mary Lee to a boarding school hundreds of miles away from home. Mary Lee is devastated:

'Try to understand,' said her mother brokenly.
   But Mary Lee had no use for that instruction. 'What is there to understand? You are ripping us away from our own selves.'
   'Listen to your phrasing, Mary Lee. Madrigal is not *your* self,' said Mother. 'She is *her* self. We have allowed ourselves and the world to treat you as a unit. We were wrong. You are not one. You are two.' (4)

Believing herself to be the less-loved of the two girls, the intensity of Mary Lee's feelings of pain and loss conveyed throughout the chapters set in the boarding school approximate to a sense of bereavement. When Madrigal flies out to visit her, Mary Lee wishes to be her: 'I wish for Madrigal's life' (20). A wish-fulfilment narrative, *Twins* immediately punishes Mary Lee for her rash wish and Madrigal is killed on the ski slopes.

   Now genuinely bereaved Mary Lee takes her sister's identity, noting later 'It was a human fantasy to remain on earth after death. To see what it was like when you no longer existed. See how people felt about you. Measure the space you left behind' (68–9). Quite soon, however, Mary Lee realizes that Madrigal had been evil, and that her parents had sent her away because they loved her more, not less. Madrigal's boyfriend, Jon Pear, now Mary Lee's boyfriend, is also depicted as evil, and the final evaluation of him stresses the lack of a supernatural dimension to his character: 'What he was was bad. Not a mirage, not a ghost, not a vampire, but a completely bad person' (156). Interestingly, particularly when compared to Stine's Point Horror fiction, he is not depicted as insane either. Despite this denial of the supernatural, *Twins* is not without aspects which, generically, place the novel between the fairy story and the fable. The novel opens with a direct allusion to Sleeping Beauty:

> Each swing of hair, each lift of brow, was mirrored in her identical twin. If it had been a fairy tale, and one twin had said, 'Mirror, Mirror on the Wall, Who Is the Fairest of Them All?' the mirror could have made no answer. For *two* qualified. (1)

Later, when Mary Lee gazes at Jon Pear, who is always given his full name, presumably to evoke the word 'apple', she wishes to kiss him 'until they both died of exhaustion, like a fairy tale in which lovers dance themselves to a frenzied end' (86–7). Similarly, her wish for the life of her sister is immediately gratified, and just as immediately punished. The girls' ability to communicate through telepathy is also clearly 'uncanny': '*Mary Lee*, came a pulsing wordless communication. *Come.* Madrigal was calling. The lovely unspoken words had returned' (31).

Twins is a self-referential fable about the necessary destruction of childish solipsism and narcissism. Tougher than anything of Stine's in the Point Horror series, *Twins* endorses the death of that regressive part of the psyche which thinks only of its self and its pleasures. The horror at the centre of the book, as in *Night School*, is the impoverishment of the spirit which occurs when the individual looks only within the self, and not at the larger world outside.

All the Point Horror supernatural novels work actually to reinstate boundaries, to formalize them, and to insist that differences do exist. The novels assert that without difference there can be no meaning; indeed that meaning is predicated upon the existence of difference. Jean Baudrillard writes on the subject of initiation: 'Initiation is the accented beat of the operation of the symbolic ... It is the *splitting* of life and death that initiation conjures away, and with it the concomitant fatality which weighs down on life as soon as it is split in this way.'[28] Baudrillard perceives initiation as a process which incorporates the initiate into a holistic universe, one which elides the distinction between life and death. Cooney's supernatural stories offer the adolescent reader a flicker of animism, and the presence of the uncanny. They depict a world that still contains magic, the omnipotence of thought, and the return of the dead. Stine's Point Horror thrillers, conversely, initiate their readers into a desacralized world which is structured around the existence of oppositions, primarily the one believed to exist between the living and the dead. Stine's thrillers resist initiation in Baudrillard's sense, while Cooney's supernatural novels promote just this understanding of initiation. Stine's fiction indulges adolescent narcissism, while Cooney's work rejects it. The thrillers invite the adolescent reader to recognize the authority of the adult world, a world where the value of the intellect or the spirit is negligible, where poverty is so unacceptable that working oneself into an early grave is the only other option, a world so mechanical, so rational, and so terrified by the idea of death as an inevitable natural process, that it will not even recognize its existence. It would be unfair to blame these books for the specious messages about death which they send; they are, after all, preparing their readers for incorporation into an adult world which also views the natural process of death as unmentionable.

Websites
Readers interested in Point Horror might find the following sites of interest:

Point Horror
http://www.scholastic.co.uk/zo (*Infoseek*)

Welcome to – Point Horror
http://matrix.crosswinds.net/-pointhorror/ (*AltaVista*)

R. L. Stine books list
http://www.webdesk.com/ristine/booklist.html (*AltaVista*)

Notes
1. A. Billen (1996) 'Little shocks for horrors', *The Observer*, 25 February.
2. Billen, *ibid.*
3. Clive Bloom (ed.) (1993) *Creepers: British Horror and Fantasy in the Twentieth Century*. London: Pluto Press, p. 124.
4. Peter Hunt (1991) *Criticism, Theory, & Children's Literature*. Oxford: Blackwell, p. 48.
5. Sigmund Freud (1978) *The Complete Psychological Works of Sigmund Freud*, vol.

XV11 (trans. James Strachey). London: The Hogarth Press, p. 220.
6. Steven King (1991) *Danse Macabre*. London: Futura, p. 48.
7. Charles Sarland (1994) 'Attack of the Teenage Horrors: Theme and Meaning in Popular Series Fiction', *Signal*, 73, p. 50.
8. J. B. Twitchell (1985) *Dreadful Pleasures: An Anatomy of Modern Horror*. Oxford: Oxford University Press, p. 85.
9. King, *op. cit.*, p. 27.
10. Bloom, *op. cit.*, p. xi.
11. Billen, *op. cit.*
12. David Charter (1998) 'Top children's author makes chilling reading', *The Times*, 26 August.
13. Twitchell, *op. cit.*, p. 19.
14. Billen, *op. cit.*
15. A. Billen (1996) 'Little horror', *The Observer*, 6 October.
16. O. Craig (1995) 'Horror and Aga sagas see romance off the shelves', *The Sunday Times*, 26 August.
17. Sarland, *op. cit.*, p. 54.
18. King, *op. cit.*, p. 66.
19. Sarland, *op. cit.*, pp. 59–60.
20. Freud, *op. cit.*, p. 224.
21. *Ibid.*, p. 234.
22. *Ibid.*, p. 220.
23. King, *op. cit.*, p. 305.
24. Freud, *op. cit.*, p. 234.
25. *Ibid.*, p. 235.
26. *Ibid.*, p. 234.
27. *Ibid.*, p. 247.
28. Jean Baudrillard (1993) *Symbolic Exchange and Death* (trans. I. Hamilton Grant). London: Sage, p. 132.

CHAPTER 2

Robert Westall's 'Frightening Fictions'

Kevin McCarron

No passion so effectually robs the mind of all its powers of acting and reasoning as fear.
Edmund Burke

Robert Westall was born in 1929 on Tyneside, where he grew up during the Second World War. He spent two years with the Royal Signals between studying Fine Art at Durham University, and Sculpture at the Slade in London. He then taught art in schools in the north of England. He was also branch director of the Samaritans, a journalist and an antique dealer. His son, Chris, was killed in a motorcycle accident in 1978. Between 1985 and his death in 1993 he was a full-time author. Antiques, art, Tyneside, and the relationships between fathers and their sons are all central preoccupations of Westall's writing.

At the time of his death Robert Westall had published almost 50 books, a large number of which could be described as 'frightening fictions', although it is erroneous to classify Westall, as is often done, as essentially a writer of ghost stories. His published work can be usefully divided, more or less neatly, into three major categories: Adventure Fiction, such as *The Machine Gunners* and *The Kingdom By the Sea*; Fiction for Juniors, which would include whimsical stories and fables such as *The Christmas Cat* and *The Christmas Ghost*; and Fearful Fiction, which can itself be subdivided into two broad categories: 'realistic' but unsettling narratives, such as 'The Bus Stop', 'Sergeant Nice', and *Gulf*; and supernatural novels and stories, such as *The Watch Tower*, *The Scarecrows*, 'The Stones of Muncaster Cathedral', and *The Wheatstone Pond*. It is beyond the scope of a study such as this to evaluate in depth all of Westall's fearful fictions; instead, given the extent of his *oeuvre*, I want to discuss, in some detail, at least fifteen of the best known of them, alluding to others throughout, including both the whimsical and the adventure stories.

It is important to note at the outset that Westall's novels and stories are written for a young audience, and to further note that while they may not generate fear in adult readers, they are clearly designed to do just this to an adolescent audience. Horror fiction is unusual in terms of genre in that its identification, unlike that of, say, detective fiction, is not structural, but visceral – horror is a literature of affect. The sheer physicality of horror's appeal is, I believe, one of the principal reasons it is consumed so avidly by adolescents. Horror is, of course, the pre-eminent adolescent genre: textually, cinematically, and televisually, and the viscerality of its effects finds a welcome response in an adolescent audience whose own bodies are beginning to change in ways that are both gratifying and disturbing. Conversely, detective fiction, in essence a cerebral genre, appeals considerably more to a mature audience, whose bodies having settled, so to speak, now give priority to mind over body. A fondness for horror is entirely appropriate in adolescents, but perhaps perverse in adults. In *The Philosophy of Horror* Noel Carroll itemizes some of the common responses reported by those who read, or watch, narratives which are clearly designed to create sensations of fear in the audience:

> In respect to art-horror some of the regularly recurring sensations, or felt-physical agitations, or automatic responses, or feelings are muscular contractions, tension, cringing, shrinking, shuddering, recoiling, tingling, frozenness, momentary arrests, chilling (hence, 'spine-chilling'), paralysis, trembling, nausea, a reflex of apprehension or physically heightened alertness (a danger response), perhaps involuntary screaming, and so on.[1]

Generally, the adult reader of adolescent 'fearful fictions', who may experience none of the responses Carroll lists above, is forced to rely on anecdotal evidence that, say, Westall's 'The Call' or *The Watch House*, are 'terrifying', but is also able to recognize certain structural motifs that justify appellations such as 'horrifying', 'terrifying', or 'frightening'.

A striking feature of Westall's writing, however, is the way in which his primary motifs and concerns, among them cats, clocks, World Wars I and II, time travel, antiques, the seaside, ghosts, dreams, religion, officialdom, aliens, gender specificity, machinery, and death appear throughout all three categories of his fiction: adventure, whimsy, and horror. Westall does not have a specific horror register, or a recurring collection of specifically fearful motifs; instead, his persistent narrative preoccupations are, to a large extent, innocent of categories: cats or clocks are just as likely to appear in a charming fable like *The Christmas Cat*, or a splendid piece of whimsy such as *If Cats Could Fly*, as they are in fearful fictions such as *Yaxley's Cat* or *The Scarecrows*.

There is little dissension among critics of the horror genre, with the pervasive view being that the genre is never actually concerned with its ostensible subject. In the introduction to *A Dark Night's Dreaming* Tony Magistrale and Michael Morrison state emphatically: 'Much of what occurs in horror art is symbolic; that is, its deepest meanings exist on a subtextual level.'[2] According to Noel Carroll, 'The horror story can be conceptualized as a symbolic defense of a culture's standards of normality ... '[3] Similarly, in Stephen King's view, we should,

> Begin by assuming that the tale of horror, no matter how primitive, is allegorical by its very nature; that it is symbolic. Assume that it is talking to us, like a patient on a psychoanalyst's couch, about one thing while it means another.[4]

The assumption that horror is, in essence, a strategy of displacement is surely true of much, even most, horror, and particularly true of the Point Horror series, as discussed in Chapter 1. However, it is not necessarily true of Westall's frightening fictions.

It will be useful for an appreciation of Westall's horror fiction to consider briefly several of his best-known adventure stories, noting motifs which not only recur, but are developed throughout his frightening fictions. Westall uses horror scenarios to accelerate the learning process for his protagonists, and it is invariably this learning process, usually from a state of spoiled superiority to one of empathy, which is his primary concern. Fear, for Westall, is an essentializing tool, and one of its primary functions is to hasten the growth of his protagonists. In addition, and no less importantly, it is rare for a ghost or a demon in Westall's work to be revealed as imaginary, or fraudulent, or capable of being explained away in a thoroughly rational expository coda. Ghosts exist in Westall's world, as does a fluid, non-linear temporality. Westall's frightening fiction is a critique of the reductive, scientific rationalism of the last half of the twentieth century.

The Machine Gunners (1975), Robert Westall's first published novel, and winner of the Carnegie Medal, features many of the issues that preoccupied him throughout his unusually prolific writing career. The novel is set in Tyneside, in the north-east of England, during the period 1940–1, when the German bombing raids were at their fiercest.

The plot of the novel is as straightforward as any of his subsequent adventure stories. Chas McGill, who has the second best collection of war souvenirs in Garmouth, and his friends find a crashed German Heinkel with a machine gun and 2000 rounds of live ammunition. The police and the Home Guard know the gun has been 'liberated' and the book follows the successful attempts of the children to outwit the authorities. In the course of the novel, the group of friends capture and subsequently befriend the German pilot, learning in the process that he is not a fiend but a human being, much like them, at the mercy of authoritarian forces he only dimly comprehends. Chas McGill and his friends reappear in several later Westall novels and stories and, significantly for this discussion, one of these, 'The Haunting of Chas McGill', propels its protagonist from the world of adventure and mimetic realism into one of portents, dreams, and ghosts. This shift is anticipated in *The Machine Gunners*. When Chas and his father visit Chas's grandparents, his grandfather recounts his most persistent dream:

> 'I dreamt he came back for his badge.'
> *He* was an Austrian soldier whom Granda had killed in a bayonet-fight at Caparetto. Granda had taken the badge as a trophy; and ever since had dreams that the dead man came back and mutely asked for his possessions. Granda had lived in fear of that man for twenty-five years ... (59)

Later, however, Chas's friend, Nicky, escapes from his house before it is bombed because his dead father appears to him in a dream and warns him of what is about to happen. The dead in Westall's work often act as advisors and guides, which is in marked distinction to the Point Horror series in which the dead are only ever represented as malevolent.

The Machine Gunners also emphasizes several other issues which recur throughout Westall's work. Chas begins the book contemptuous of families living in council housing: 'Chas watched them as if they were ants, without sympathy, because they were a slummy kind of family ...' (10). However, consistent with Westall's work overall, Chas begins to understand and sympathize with others by the novel's conclusion. Mr McGill, a fitter, who 'made things to last' (105), is the first in a very long line of Westall's male characters who are enthralled by machinery, and who respect the past as manifested in well-made, beautiful objects. In the gang's wonderfully cosy hide-out, the Fortress, the children draw up a list of thirteen Standing Orders, amusing in themselves but which also clearly parody similar regulations in Mark Twain's *The Adventures of Tom Sawyer* and *Huckleberry Finn*. Overall there is considerable humour of a predominantly intertextual nature, which, it must be assumed, is rarely recognized by the adolescent reader.

Fathom Five (1979) is also set in Garmouth, but it is now 1943 and Chas McGill has moved away, although most of the old gang remain. Like *The Machine Gunners*, *Fathom Five* is a straightforward adventure novel, in which Jack, Audrey, Cem, and Sheila track down a spy who is passing vital information to the Germans about Allied ships entering and leaving the harbour. Again, many of Westall's most persistent concerns can be found in *Fathom Five*. Jack's parents, amiable male and snappy status-conscious female, are reproduced in various forms throughout Westall's writing. Jack's love of trawling the beach: 'You could always find something smelly and interesting washed up on the Sands' (5), is emulated by dozens of Westall's subsequent characters, always boys. This love of objects, and a concomitant animism, is a striking feature of Westall's work, and it is a rare Westall novel which does not contain an extensive list of *objets trouvés*, many of which, in the horror narratives, have supernatural powers. The novel also has many comic moments, some of which are unlikely to be appreciated by the adolescent reader: 'Mam dreaded gambling. One of her brothers had Ruined Himself at Cards and Died Young' (14). In *Fathom Five* Jack learns the same important lesson as Chas did in *The Machine Gunners* – sympathy: 'Riding round the town, whenever he saw slummy places or slummy kids, he didn't despise them anymore – he saw them as victims of the Smythsons' (161–2). Jack's father, like Chas's, and like a host of Westall's male characters, is technically adept, while Audrey, now a young woman, becomes the first of a series of Westall's female characters whose physical and emotional growth far outpaces that of her male contemporaries. This issue becomes central to the supernatural narratives, where, invariably, it is the female characters who detect the presence of the uncanny while the males are still busy attempting to explain away mysteries by recourse to science and logic. Westall is comfortable with such stereotypical representations, and goes further, often establishing connections between the female and the feline, stressing their shared intuitive powers, sensual appetites, and their capacity for cruelty and violence.

Blitzcat (1989) won the Smarties award in 1989. As the title suggests, *Blitzcat* centres on the most ubiquitous presence in all of Westall's fiction – cats. The novel traces the journey of a cat, Lord Gort, from the blazing ruins of bombed-out Coventry throughout the South of England and parts of France searching for her master. Westall focuses on the telepathic powers of the cat, so intense as to verge on the supernatural, as well as its indomitability, loyalty, and courage. The cat becomes a symbol of the English themselves during the war, and Westall weaves the animal in and out of people's lives, all of whom are changed by the cat's presence. In perhaps the most memorable episode, a young woman novelist, whose husband has been killed at sea, and who is clearly in the process of killing herself through self-neglect in her grief, is brought back to life by her desire to stop the cat dying of cold and hunger. The cat becomes a creature, never other than the protagonist of a mimetically realistic fiction who bridges the worlds between life and death. As Susan watches the now healthy cat with her kitten, her husband briefly comes back to life: 'And just for a second he seemed to be in her mind, like a tiny bright spark. She knew without doubt that he was dead, but she equally knew without doubt that he still existed, somewhere, and was pleased with her' (167). In Westall's work, cats are part of the domestic scenery and simultaneously inhabitants of a secret, violent world. They are cruel, sensuous, intuitive, telepathic, mysterious and, ultimately, unknowable. They are absolutely central to Westall's horror fiction.

The Kingdom By the Sea (1990) won *The Guardian* Children's Fiction award in 1991. It is set during the early years of World War II, in Northumberland, with an extended sequence set on Lindisfarne. *The Kingdom By the Sea* is a picaresque novel, which recounts the wanderings of its protagonist, Harry, as he travels along the Northumbrian coast after a bombing raid, during which he believes his parents have been killed. The primary motivation for his travels is to escape having to live with his cousin Elsie who 'was more awful than death itself' (11). The novel contains several of Westall's characteristic preoccupations: World War II, animals, the amiability of men compared to women, the development of sympathy in the protagonist, and the masculine enjoyment of engineering. There are also some splendid sequences describing objects washed up on the beach:

> He found a penny, with the King's head almost worn away by the sea and sand. He found a round rusty tin, still half-full of sweet-smelling tobacco. He found a sodden navy-blue jumper, with one elbow worn out, but it would darn. A baby's dummy, nearly new, a deflated rubber bathing-ring that could be repaired. Two crabs stranded by the tide, a dead flatfish that was sniffed and pronounced still fresh, and a crippled sea-bird that he despatched with one blow of a charred plank, saying it would make supper, but he was most jubilant about some orangey stones, that he said were amber. (66)

Although *The Kingdom By the Sea* is an adventure story, it is worth noting that in another of Westall's novels any of the inorganic objects described here could initiate a 'time slip' narrative, or prove a gateway to the world of the supernatural. The novel ends with Harry discovering his parents are alive and being forced to return to them, although he would rather stay with Mr M. and his 'kingdom by the sea'. It is an impressively sombre ending, rather as though Huckleberry Finn had been forced to return to the Widder Douglas. Westall sounds an interesting ambivalence here, as much of the novel is taken up with Harry's longing to be reunited with his family, of whom he is initially accepting and uncritical. Harry's grief is displaced by adventure and, in effect, his family's 'return from the dead' is as disturbing to him as if they had been ghosts.

In *A Place For Me* (1993) the protagonist, Lucy, is sent into hiding by her father, who is a 'whistle blower', about to inform the Press of the Government's complicity in dumping toxic waste. This novel, too, contains a large number of Westall's preoccupations: the single-parent family, antiques, cats, the male love of technology and construction, and, most strikingly, clocks. Indeed, it is Lucy's love of a beautiful old clock, and her refusal of a very large sum of money for it, that saves her life. Throughout Westall's work characters learn both sympathy for other people and respect for the creative achievements of the past. Clocks are Westall's favourite objects for linking aesthetics with time, and time is a primary concern of his supernatural fiction.

> *A satisfactory spook should have a metabolism, a purpose and a modus operandi.*
>
> Robert Westall, *The Watch Tower*

> *The relationship between truth, belief and legend has never been thoroughly explored. Too much faith certainly leads to gullibility; but perhaps too much scepticism leads to undue blindness.*
>
> Robert Westall, *The Wind Eye*

The Wind Eye (1976) is a 'time slip' narrative, a variant on the more conventional historical novel commonly employed by Westall. The principal structural device of such narratives is juxtaposition of the present and the past, but Westall adds to this by alternating between different narrative perspectives. Technically, it is a very accomplished novel, although this is only one of its attributes. 'Time slip' narratives are not usually perceived as generating fear; however, it can safely be assumed that the way in which conventional distinctions between the past, present, and future are elided in such narratives is unsettling for the reader. Indeed, it may actually be the case that Westall's eerie and almost seamless shifts from the past to the present, from the 'real' to the 'unreal', are considerably more frightening to many adolescent readers than any number of formulaic horror clichés. The anxiety generated by such narratives is, structurally, and even philosophically, similar to that created by ghost stories: in both forms of narrative a distinction previously believed to be obvious and permanent is emphatically rejected. In the 'time slip' narrative the distinction between past and present is elided and in the ghost story the clear demarcation line separating the living from the dead is depicted as not at all permanent and universal, but rather as fluid and unpredictable, and by no means amenable to the laws of science. This issue is, in essence, epistemological, and forms part of the learning process undergone by so many of Westall's protagonists. Such lessons, however, are not offered overtly, in the form of obviously uplifting dialogue, or thematically, in the form of recognizable injunctions conveyed by the reward and punishment configurations of the story, but are structural, embedded in the mode of exposition itself. Not only does Westall respect the past, and invite his readers to do the same, but, perhaps more impressively, he is constantly alert to its brutality. *The Wind Eye* offers a good example of this:

> Next moment the leader raised his sword and hacked the lad's head from his shoulders. Blood from the severed neck spouted over Bertrand's sandalled feet. It was shockingly hot. The poor head lay on its side, mouth twitching slightly as if it was still alive. (183–4)

The Wind Eye opens with marital discord; he, Bertrand, is a decent, liberal academic, stunted by his excessive rationalism, while his wife, Madeline, is untidy, irresponsible and emotionally unpredictable. At the novel's conclusion, both have ameliorated their views, but Bertrand has learned more, and, accordingly, he has changed more. The family: Bertrand, Madeline, Michael, Madeline's son from a previous marriage, Beth and Sally, Bertrand's children from his previous marriage, are to have a holiday at Monk's Heugh, which is in a remote part of the Northumbrian coast, and has been in the family for generations, but has been empty since Uncle Henry died. Symbolically, they set off in two cars, and break their journey at Durham Cathedral, where Madeline deliberately tramples on the tomb of St Cuthbert. Monk's Heugh, the family later discovers, is directly opposite the Farne Islands, where St Cuthbert once lived – thirteen hundred years earlier. The children find a boat, the *Ressure*, which they soon find is capable of transporting them back in time to when St Cuthbert was alive. Central to the plot is the miraculous healing of Sally's hand, deformed in a domestic accident, and it is this miracle, performed by St Cuthbert, which finally convinces Bertrand that his rational approach to the universe needs to be reappraised.

The use of a specific object necessary for time travel, in this case the *Ressure*, is a characteristic feature of Westall's work; things often possess a talismanic power in his writing, and many of the supernatural stories begin with the discovery of an old object which often possesses the primary attributes of its most famous historical owner, for better or worse. Several other features in *The Wind Eye*, such as the stonemasons at Durham Cathedral and a sleepwalking child, appear elsewhere in Westall's supernatural fiction.

Both somnambulism and stonemasons are central to the plot of the very powerful story 'The Stones of Muncaster Cathedral', as is religion, always a pervasive presence in Westall's fiction, and particularly important to *The Wind Eye*. In this novel Westall displays a sophisticated grasp of the complex interplay between wrath and redemption in Christianity. Although no character in the novel is able to answer Beth's perplexed question: ' "Why is Cuddy so violent? I thought saints were gentle and loving" ' (203), throughout *The Wind Eye* Westall displays a keen understanding of the violence at the centre of Christianity, and, unusually, for a contemporary writer, he does not reject this religious violence in favour of tolerance and understanding. Instead, the irrational, supernatural violence of Cuddy is clearly preferred to the blinkered rationalism of Bertrand, who joins a long list of Westall's male protagonists who learn that the world is by no means always governed by rational forces. While it would not be completely accurate to suggest that Bertrand, like others of Westall's male characters, becomes 'feminized' in the course of the narrative, it is certainly the case that Westall does stress throughout his work the female capacity for intuition and the desirability of learning to accept that there may be alternative explanations for phenomena and behaviour we either think we already understand or which we simply discount. This issue is almost certainly linked to his preoccupation with death, and, strikingly, becomes more fully developed in his work after the death of his son in 1978. The central issue here may well be the articulation of an inchoate desire to be reunited after death, despite what reason and experience teach.

On the front cover of the 1995 edition of *The Watch House* (1977), *Junior Bookshelf* is quoted: 'A great ghost story. One of the best ever.' Certainly, it is eerie and evocative. It is a contemporary novel, set in the fictitious Garmouth, which, as Westall acknowledges in an afterword, is actually Tynemouth. The novel opens with Anne, the adolescent protagonist, being left with her mother's old nanny, Prudie, for the summer. The name 'Prudie', clearly short for Prudence, establishes the older woman's character immediately, and informs readers that they are engaged in a narrative which is as much symbolic as it is realistic. It is rapidly established that Anne's parents' marriage is over, and characteristically within Westall's work, that Anne's mother is vain, mean-spirited, and promiscuous, while her father is weak, but amiable. In the course of her stay, Anne encounters a ghost in the Watch House, which looks out over the coast and from which the lifeboats are called out. The Watch House itself is described in language which reconstructs the building in human terms:

> The road ended at the Watch House, which loomed over them as they got out of the car. Built of long white planks, sagging with the years, it had a maritime look. Like a mastless roofed-in schooner becalmed in a sea of dead grass. Single-storey like a church hall. Through its windows showed a dark clutter of things that couldn't be recognized. This clutter and lack of curtains made the windows look like eyes in a white planked face. (5)

Westall's work is full of such powerful images, and he is particularly adroit at constructing evocative and striking similes. In *The Wind Eye*, for example, after St Cuthbert has created the storm that decimates the Vikings, Westall writes: 'Sea and land seemed to have changed places. For the sea was afloat with land-things; uprooted bushes and dead sheep. Whereas the shore where they landed was buried in seaweed, already steaming and stinking in the sun. It had an awesome deep smell, as if the sea had vomited' (195). In *The Watch House* a succession of images immediately invests the buildings and the landscape with recognizably human qualities: 'The headland on the left was red sandstone, with red sandstone ruins on top. Ruins like crumbling hands, with fingers pointing skywards ... Below the ruins, on the incredibly green grass, huddled an army of tombstones ... ' (4). Linguistic stratagems such as these blur the distinction between inorganic and organic, and anticipate the novel's later blurring of past and present, living and dead.

Generically, the novel is both ghost story and 'time slip' narrative, with the latter plunging Anne back in time so she can witness the brutal act of murder which has caused the ghost's return from the dead. Tension is cleverly built throughout this section as Westall describes Anne's anxieties and her fear. As is characteristic of Westall's 'time slip' narratives, he lays a strong, and salutary, emphasis on the violence of the past, noting, in particular, the murderous lengths to which wreckers and looters would go to in trying to extract a dishonest living from the sea. Westall is, overall, remarkably successful at conflating genres: *Gulf*, for example, is a very successful blending of war story and supernatural narrative. The Watch House is a museum and, again characteristically, Westall carefully depicts the objects retrieved from the sea which constitute its primary exhibits. It is these objects which contain historical, and ultimately, supernatural energy powerful enough to breach the laws of physics and merge the present and the past, and the living and the dead. *The Watch House*, structurally, revolves about a sequence of polarities in addition to those just noted: particularly those of sea and land, age and youth, male and female, and, more unusually, Anglicanism and Roman Catholicism.

In an episode which is absolutely typical not only of Westall's supernatural fiction, but of adolescent supernatural fiction in general, Timothy attempts to persuade Anne that the flickers she has seen at night in the Watch House are explicable by recourse to the laws of physics:

> 'I must have disturbed that wire last night,' said Timmo, after twenty minutes. 'You see, when a wire's just touching a terminal, the current passing through warms the wire, so that it expands and bends away, and the contact's lost. The wire cools, and comes back to the terminal. So you get a flicker.' (105)

To their credit, neither Anne nor her friend Pat, are in the slightest impressed by this masculine reductivism: ' "It's not that," said Pat, still sulky from last night. "It's *you*. It won't do anything while you're around" '(105). Timothy, like Bertrand in *The Wind Eye*, comes to realize that not everything in the world is reducible to scientific logic. As I mentioned earlier, religion is a very strong presence in Westall's work, as indeed it tends to be in horror writing in general, while it is completely absent from Point Horror narratives. In *The Watch House* the two priests, intriguingly, replicate the novel's gender polarities, also emulating the move from scepticism to belief. Father da Souza, foreign, Catholic, and sympathetic to Anne's belief in ghosts, is gendered as female in the novel; while Father Fletcher, emphatically English, pragmatic, and sceptical, is gendered as indisputably masculine. It is important to note, however, that da Souza's religious vision, his narrative 'femininity' notwithstanding, is harsh, even cruel, and clearly at odds with Fletcher's more amiable views. In a telling exchange between the two priests, in the Watch House itself, in front of Anne, da Souza snaps at Father Fletcher:

> 'That's the trouble with you of the Church of England. You see Heaven as a kind of Welfare State, with everyone entitled to benefits. We of Rome are not so wholesale. We say *if* a man makes a good deathbed confession; *if* he receives absolution and the Last Rites, his soul goes safe to Purgatory. Do you think we give the Last Rites as a joke? Without them we make no promises.' (112)

Da Souza's harsh religious understanding is quite consistent with the depiction of Christianity in *The Wind Eye*, which, of course, predates the Church of England by hundreds of years. The typical Westall combination of harsh woman and amiable man is replicated here in religious terms.

Father Fletcher, however, like Timothy, and like Bertrand, moves from a position of hostile scepticism to one of open-mindedness by the novel's conclusion. It is common in Westall's work, and also in Point Horror narratives, that females begin with the belief in the possibility of the supernatural, while males must learn to accept it through the course of the narrative; invariably, agency is provided by the female in the masculine learning process.

The Devil On The Road was published in 1978, the year Westall's son died in a motorcycle accident. It is another 'time slip' narrative, this time sending the protagonist back in time to the seventeenth century, about 1645–47, when Matthew Hopkins, The Witch Finder General, was at his most zealous. Many of Westall's favourite motifs are to be found in *The Devil On The Road*: cats, time, machinery, gender specificity, and historical objects, and, once again, a male character learns in the course of the narrative that the world is not as easy to understand, or as rational, as he had previously assumed. John Webster, however, is not a conventional Westall male character. Certainly, he is very competent with machinery, writing of his beloved Triumph Tiger-Cub motorcycle: '[I] rebuilt her from top to bottom; high-lift cam, high-compression piston and roller-bearing crankshaft so she wouldn't blow apart. I can strip her in a day *and* put it all back. Tuned her like Yehudi Menuhin's violin' (3). Conventionally, although the terminology here is technically precise, John genders the motorcycle as female. Similarly, John announces at the beginning of the novel: 'I go looking for Lady Chance, before she comes looking for me' (2). Chance, irrational and capricious, is, like Luck, a lady. John's understanding of this already indicates that he will be responsive to a breach in the rational order – in other words, he has considerably less learning to do than the majority of Westall's male characters.

At the opening of the novel, John is beginning his first university vacation and he sets off wherever 'Lady Chance' will take him. She takes him to an old barn in Suffolk, where he soon notices that strange symbols have been gouged in one of the barn doors, and where he befriends a kitten that eerily seems to do a week's growing every day. The cat, of course, is a 'familiar', and it transports John back into the seventeenth century. Here, he meets a beautiful young woman who is accused of being a witch, and to save her life he does battle with the Witch Finder General himself. Structurally, the dominant feature of the novel is juxtaposition: the novel progresses by alternating episodes set in the present and in the seventeenth century. As is so often the case, however, structure and theme are inseparable.

The Devil On The Road is unusual in its attitude to witches for a contemporary novel. The rationalism of our own age usually suggests that witches in the supernatural sense do not exist, and have never existed, but innocent, ordinary women have been brutally tortured and murdered by people like Hopkins over the centuries using witchcraft as the excuse. The motives of those who persecuted witches may have been religious, financial, or sadistic (or all three), but our age takes for granted that their victims were never really witches. Westall's novel, however, suggests that many such women really were witches, but that they should not have been harmed because of this.

On his frustrating, traffic-ensnarled way out of London at the beginning of the novel, John exclaims: 'Suddenly I hated the whole bloody twentieth century' (6). This comment is the primary reason he is sent back in time. As noted earlier, he has less learning to do about the existence of the irrational in the universe than the great majority of Westall's male protagonists, but he still has much to learn about the twentieth century itself. Westall has said:

> On the whole children don't read historical novels anymore. They don't want to know what the seventeenth century said to the seventeenth, but they become quite interested in what the twentieth century might have to say to the seventeenth. I feel able, with research, to let the twentieth century talk to the seventeenth, and to see the seventeenth as an observer.[5]

What is particularly impressive about Westall's use of history is the aspect of it he invariably fixes upon: its brutality. It is possible that the young reader of such narratives is responding to and appropriating a sublimated evolutionary model of historical development: these narratives demonstrate a movement from ignorance to enlightenment;

one which, presumably Westall hoped, would be replicated in the reader.

Perhaps more importantly, however, Westall has virtually no interest in having characters offer synopses of important political or military events, nor does he bother overmuch with dates. The didactic drive underlying his historical representations is, arguably, considerably more important than the simple imparting of historical facts; his primary concern is to demonstrate to young readers how fortunate they are to be living in a civilized, humane society. John is 'horrified' at the ignorant and rapacious brutality of the seventeenth century, and a similar lesson is learned by all of Westall's time travellers, irrespective of the manner in which the characters become aware of the past. In the short story 'The Bus' (1988) Jack is bitterly contemptuous of contemporary England, until the bus becomes a time machine, taking Jack back through the recent decades of England's history, disclosing to him the racism, poverty, ignorance, and violence of those years; at the story's conclusion he asks the driver to return him to his own time. *The Christmas Cat* (1991) is constructed as a monologue addressed to the narrator's granddaughter, and a central feature of the story is its recreation of the grinding poverty of the 1930s:

> You cannot imagine, granddaughter, the sights I saw that day. Groups of unemployed men, squatting at the street corners, passing round the flattened dog-end of a cigarette from one to the other; smoking it, with the aid of a pin stuck through it until it was only a quarter inch long. A man with no legs, just flat worn black leather pads where his legs should be, singing carols in a deep sweet voice from a doorstep, with his little dog nearby and a flat cap into which some passers-by put halfpennies. (50)

The opening phrase here, 'You cannot imagine', is no rhetorical flourish, not when addressed to a young, contemporary reader who has grown up in a Welfare State. However, while Westall is always concerned to show his young readers just how brutal the past was, he is equally persistent in drawing attention to the imaginative impoverishment of contemporary civilized society, and his most successful work is often generated by the inevitable tension existing between these two positions.

The Scarecrows (1981) won the Carnegie Medal in 1982, making Westall the first writer to win it twice, and he remains the only double winner. It is an extremely impressive novel, particularly in the way it uses a frightening fiction to articulate a profound moral about death, hate, and grief. Generically it is a ghost story, but this is only half the story. The dead are transformed into scarecrows, emerging organically out of their rural setting, manifesting themselves as beings capable of effecting change in the world of the living. However, *The Scarecrows* is simultaneously a novel about the way in which a real, fallible, living stepfather replaces an idealized, perfect dead father. The ingenuity of the novel resides primarily in the way in which the domestic drama drives the ghost story – the protagonist's determined hatred for his stepfather is what summons the dead back to life. The malicious dead are nurtured by hatred.

The plot, as always, is straightforward. While reluctantly spending the summer at his stepfather's house in the country, Simon stumbles upon an old mill house. A newspaper shows the mill has been abandoned since 1943, but it creates an inexplicable sense of unease in the troubled adolescent. With the help of local newspapers Simon is able to discover the horrible story of betrayal and murder which took place at the mill, and he gradually realizes that the dead have come back with evil intent, as scarecrows. Simon's surname, 'Wood', has conventionally been read in England since Shakespeare as 'mad', and certainly Simon is mad – mad with hate. His beloved father, a fit, smart, soldier killed on active service in Aden, has been replaced by a stepfather, Joe Moreton, who is presented to the reader through Simon's eyes as an overweight, slovenly artist. As the novel progresses, Simon learns that his dead father was cold and hard, offering another possible interpretation of his name, while he begins to see that his stepfather is warm and amiable. Again, we see Westall's favourite polarity, this time imposed upon two men, as it was in *The Watch House*, but here one of the men is dead and the other is alive.

Several of Westall's other preoccupations are present in *The Scarecrows* too, particularly antiques and cats, but absolutely central to the novel is the mill, and Simon becomes a typical Westall male protagonist in his fascination with how the machinery of the mill operates:

> The vertical main drive shaft caught his eye, with the great grinding millstone at the bottom. An octagonal oak pillar, with a huge wooden cog fastened horizontally across the top. Struts went up from the shaft to support the cog; diagonally, like the diagonal strut on a gallows. But he was far more interested in the way the cog fitted into the next cog, which fitted into the next shaft, which had another cog ... He began to understand how the mill worked. Understanding, he climbed slowly upwards to the very top platform. (63)

It is a mark of Simon's despair, frustration, and grief for his father that he smashes something he finds so fascinating. The masculine fascination with machinery and engineering, ubiquitous in Westall's work, might suggest to some adult readers that at least some of his appeal for young male readers lies in such detailed depictions of machinery. Conversely, it is also assumed that female readers are less interested in machinery and respond more favourably to the relationships between characters. The female response, inevitably, receives more cultural approbation. However, the assumption underlying this polarity: that young males enjoy technical detail as an end in itself, doing nothing with it, so to speak, while the females learn from the depiction of relationships and integrate the lessons into their own lives, may well be meretricious. It is worth considering the possibility that this fascination with machinery is, in essence, aesthetic. It is the beauty of the well-designed machine which is being celebrated at such moments, but, and Westall always stresses this point, beautiful machinery stands apart from the horror and the bloodshed which has accompanied human progress. A perfectly constructed object in Westall's work, be it a painting, a clock, or a machine, is a statement about human creativity and potential and is to be valued for this reason, not because it reflects and sustains a masculine and infantile preoccupation with toys. Gradually, Simon sees that his stepfather's care for his own work is worthy of respect. Westall also implies in *The Scarecrows* that the mill's machinery was made by someone who cared, that love has gone into its construction, and it is this recognition that eventually helps him to love his dead father no less, but also assists him in attempting to love his stepfather as well. As he makes this attempt, the scarecrows are defeated.

The novel's most successful aspect, however, may be the way in which the persistence of the dead is examined. In a powerful and disturbing scene, Simon leaves his father's army uniform on a chair in his mother's and Joe's bedroom, and after they discover it, he tells his mother: ' "I cleaned Father's kit and put it there. To remind you he still exists, you whore" ' (91). Not surprisingly, Simon longs for his dead father to come back to life again. The scarecrows present him with three people who have come back from the dead, and stress their monstrous and horrifying unnaturalness. Simon learns in the course of the novel that the dead should not come back to life, that life must continue without them, and must contain love, not hate, but he also learns that the dead do not cease to exist if they do not return as ghosts; they live as benign memories, still capable of determining our choices and constructing our morality. The dead, ideally, have agency, but not corporeality. Such an understanding of the dead is totally absent from Point Horror narratives, where the only decent action that can be performed by the dead is to pretend that they never existed. In Westall's work, the dead can be beneficent guides, as in *The Scarecrows* and *The Machine Gunners*, but in Point Horror the dead are only ever agents of horror. *The Scarecrows* addresses a number of adolescent fears, notably parental death and abandonment, and does so within a narrative that is tense and disturbing. The oppressive and ominous silence of the scarecrows and their inexorable movement towards the house is fearful, but particularly so because the supernatural horror reflects the social drama which, in turn, animates it.

Break of Dark (1982) is a collection of five stories: 'Hitch-hiker', 'Blackham's Wimpey', 'Fred, Alice and Aunty Lou', 'St. Austin Friars', and 'Sergeant Nice'. The first and last of these stories feature aliens, a subject which recurs periodically, and not always particularly successfully, throughout Westall's *oeuvre*, perhaps culminating in the extraordinary novel *Urn Burial*. Alien narratives, like 'time slip' narratives, are not so much horrifying as unsettling: they introduce an element of unpredictability into the world and suggest to the young reader that anything is possible – even in a rational world that does not accept the possibility of the supernatural. In this sense, alien stories are transitional texts, occupying a generic ground between mimetic realism, because the power of aliens is commensurate with their logic, if not ours, and stories of the supernatural.

'Hitch-hiker' exemplifies another form of narrative that regularly occurs in Westall's fiction: the wish-fulfilment story. Clearly derived from the fairy story, the wish-fulfilment story invariably rebukes the protagonist's childish desire for immediate and extravagant gratification, and, structurally, is better suited to the short story than the novel. 'The Bus' is both 'time slip' narrative and wish-fulfilment story, and 'Hitch-hiker' is both alien story and wish-fulfilment narrative. In 'Hitch-hiker' the male protagonist, who has no money at all, encounters a beautiful, naked woman while hitch-hiking:

> A girl was standing there, stark naked, her arms crossed across her breasts, looking at me with exactly the air of a startled deer. God, she was a smasher. Long silky blond hair, long shapely legs, slightly cut and bleeding in one place from the bracken-stems. Even with her arms crossed where they were, I could see that *Men Only* had nothing on her. It was, I suppose, every adolescent's wish-fulfilment. (3)

She is more than happy to sleep with him, and, no less importantly, she also has an uncanny ability to pick winners at the racetrack. Westall clearly offers this situation: more money than the narrator can spend, and uncomplicated sex with a beautiful blonde woman, as an adolescent fantasy, every red-blooded boy's wish come true. However, when the mysterious lover gives birth to triplets, who grow unnaturally quickly, like the kitten in *The Devil On The Road*, it becomes apparent to the narrator that she is an alien. His disenchantment soon turns to fear, and eventually he manages to escape. She tries to kill him by running him over in their van but goes over the cliff, taking all the money with her. The narrator's last words to the implied male reader are hortatory: 'If you see any naked blondes towards evening, mate, just bloody run' (29).

In 'Sergeant Nice' the aliens are more immediately threatening, but outwitted by human intelligence and decency. The story is not especially compelling, but has some light, comic touches which may strike a chord in some readers: 'But Constable Hughes had been dealt with fairly thoroughly. Orders to keep his eyes open for a streaker on the golf-links up the coast. "Any description?" asked Constable Hughes hungrily; he was a badly over-married man' (144).

'St. Austell Friars' anticipates *The Christmas Cat* in its depiction of a vicar unappreciated by his community, but in this case it becomes apparent that the village offers its allegiance not to Christianity, but to the Drogos, a family of vampires who control everybody in the area, the majority of whom, it is implied, are also vampires. The story also anticipates 'The Stones of Muncaster Cathedral' in its use of a church to contextualize evil, but differs strikingly, and impressively, from it, in the way that the vampires defeat the Christians. 'Fred, Alice, and Aunty Lou' is the weakest story in the collection. Generically a suburban ghost story, Westall was clearly hoping to suggest that uncanny events do not require a recognizably Gothic setting in which to occur. It is perhaps most interesting for the way in which Westall constructs another masculine polarity similar to the ones he employs in *The Scarecrows*. In this case, the two men are an unimaginative, trim, well-dressed business man, and an amiable, overweight, slovenly artist, the power of whose imagination is linked to, or even creates the ghosts. The drab presence of these ghosts, however, generates no sense of fear or horror in the reader. Westall, who was himself an art teacher as well as a writer, rarely portrays the artist in unflattering terms.

'Blackham's Wimpey' is a World War II ghost story, brilliantly evocative of its period, and, as always when Westall is writing historically, the story constantly stresses the dangers and privations of an earlier period in English history. The careful attention to technical detail in Westall's descriptions of aircraft allow the supernatural horror of the story to seem credible. Overall, the story is a beautifully judged amalgam of realism and horror. Like *The Christmas Cat* the form of the story is a recitation, but this time to a contemporary: 'Yes, I do fly in bombers. What's it like, bombing Germany? Do you really want to know? OK, brace yourself. Two more pints, please, George' (30). The expectation is that we will hear of the horrors of war and of his physical fear; this is dashed by the supernatural fear created within the story. The pub becomes the equivalent of a Victorian parlour, and the ghost story is framed by this recitative device, which, of course, means that the reader, like the implied listener, is never sure whether the story can be believed. The narrator of the story describes a quite inexplicable event, one which is horrifying in every respect. His squadron, who were returning from a bombing raid on Krefeld, were attacked by a German fighter, a Junkers 88. Flight-Sergeant Blackham's Wimpey, a Wellington bomber, shoots down the Junkers, and at that moment, according to the narrator, the laws of science are defied: 'I still don't understand what happened next. I don't think my opening up of our intercom alone could have caused it. I can only think it was some kind of electronic hiccup. But suddenly our intercom was full of alien voices' (46). Inexplicably, the narrator can hear both Blackham's intercom and the dying German screaming into his own intercom. Blackham, whose name has inevitable symbolic connotations, has already been introduced into the narrative: 'Blackham the bastard. In civvy-street, he was a Yorkshire hill farmer, a real Yorkshire tyke. Pig-ignorant and hard with it, with a hill farmer's attitude to life and death. Would send his granny to the knacker's yard, if the price was right' (41). Now, as the dying German screams for his mother, Blackham and his crew laugh at him:

> He screamed. It must have been his death scream. But then the flames must have let go of him again, like a cat lets go a half-dead mouse. We could hear him whimpering ... At least I think it was that, among the bubblings from his burnt nose and mouth and lungs. He sounded more like a half-slaughtered animal than a man; except nobody would ever do that kind of thing to an animal ... Telling his mother he didn't have a left hand anymore, that his charred fingers had broken off on the control-column. And all the time, in the background, Blackham's lot were laughing. (46–7)

The German's ghost returns to haunt the whole squadron, taking a terrible vengeance.

Perhaps the most powerful aspect of the story is the way in which it is made clear that Blackham and his crew are not haunted and hounded to their own deaths for doing their job; Westall is no pacifist. The story stresses that Blackham and his crew cannot be forgiven for the pleasure they take in killing, nor can they be forgiven for laughing at a man dying in such agony. Thematically, the story centres around that great Westall subject: sympathy. Generally Westall's work is optimistic, encouraging and rewarding the development of sympathy, but in 'Blackham's Wimpey' he works in reverse, decisively punishing so grotesque a lack of sympathy. The text engages with the reader's fear of the unknown by imaginatively conveying the increasing fear of the sensible narrator as he accepts that the squadron is being haunted by a malevolent ghost. 'Blackham's Wimpey' is not only the best story in the collection, but, with 'The Stones of Muncaster Cathedral', one of Westall's finest achievements in the short story form.

The Haunting of Chas McGill (1983) is a collection of eight stories. Three of them have no element of horror in them at all: 'The Vacancy' is a bleak fable set in the future, 'The Night Out' is another bleak story depicting a young motor cyclist's anxieties about impending domesticity and middle age, and 'The Dracula Tour', its title notwithstanding, is actually an epistolary, comic critique of horror conventions, although it is worth noting that the female narrator admits she is strongly attracted to Dracula. The remaining five horror stories, however, are among the best Westall wrote.

'The Haunting of Chas McGill' is a very understated ghost story, achieving its considerable effect by spending a large proportion of its brief length painstakingly recreating the minute details of domestic life in the very early days of World War II, before almost imperceptibly slipping into the realms of the supernatural. While staying at the Elms with his grandparents, Chas, the protagonist of Westall's first novel *The Machine Gunners*, encounters a ghost; the ghost of a soldier from the First World War, who hanged himself rather than return to the trenches. The story opens with Chas in a state of great excitement about the war:

> What a Sunday morning! Clustering round the radio at eleven o'clock, all hollow-bellied like the end of an England-Australia Test. Only this was the England-Germany Test. He had his score-cards all ready, pinned on his bedroom wall: number of German tanks destroyed; number of German planes shot down; number of German ships sunk.
>
> The Prime Minister's voice, finally crackling over the air,

seemed to Chas a total disaster. Mr Chamberlain *regretted* that a state of war now existed between England and Germany. Worse, he bleated like a sheep; or the sort of kid who, challenged in the playground, backs into a corner with his hands in front of his face and threatens to tell his Dad on you. (9)

The primary concern of the story is to teach Chas that war is not comparable to a cricket match, or to a fight between two children in a school playground. The ghost dramatizes for him something of the real horrors of war, and validates Chamberlain's 'regret'. When Chas first encounters the soldier, unaware at this time that he is a ghost from World War I, Chas is contemptuous: ' "You've got no guts," said Chas angrily. "You're a deserter" ' (27). However, the soldier tells him stories about the actuality of war, in particular the death and attempted burial of his best friend, Manny, whose name has obvious symbolic connotations:

We couldn't get Manny's body clear, so in the end we buried him respectful as we could, in the front wall o' our trench. Only the rain beat us. We got awake next morning, an' the trench wall had part-collapsed, and there was his hand sticking out, only his hand. An' no way could we get the earth to cover it again. Can ye think what that was like, passing that hand twenty times a day? But every time the lads came past they would shake hands wi' old Manny, an' wish him good morning like a gentleman. It kept you sane. Till the rats got to the hand; it was bare bone by the next morning, and gone the morning after. Aah didn't have much *guts* left after that ... (28)

Inevitably, Chas begins to sympathize with the soldier, and begins planning ways to help him escape to the countryside. Significantly, Chas sympathizes no less when he finally discovers that the soldier is a ghost.

Chas's grandparents have specialized and characteristic roles to play in this story: his grandfather tells him about the great historical battles of the First World War, while his grandmother, less aware of the political and historical context, knows the individual story of the soldier who committed suicide. Westall's fantastic fiction is often of the most disturbing sort, where there is no clear, secondary world, but the primary world is invaded by, or violated by things which 'cannot' exist. While 'The Haunting of Chas McGill' steadily builds up a sense of fear and unease in the reader, Chas's grandparents offer a recognizable sense of security. Overall, grandparents play a large part in Westall's fiction, and they still have much to teach their descendants, even, sometimes, after they are dead.

'Almost A Ghost Story' is almost as understated as 'The Haunting of Chas McGill', and remarkable for its truncated ending, which gives rise to the metafictional title. It is set in an old abbey, part of which has been transformed into a concert venue. The story opens *in media res*, immediately presenting Rachel and her mother as amenable to the possibility of ghosts existing, in particular the ghost of a nun who is rumoured to haunt the abbey, while Rachel's father is a reductive rationalist, brutally contemptuous of the very idea of ghosts. As so often the mother is querulous, and the father amiable: 'Dad laughed to himself, at the memory of being a young rip; he was never cross for long. But Mum couldn't leave him alone' (36). When Rachel goes to the toilet, terrified at the thought of encountering the nun's ghost, she receives a very unpleasant shock: 'There was a black-robed figure, standing right outside the entrance to the Ladies. Black from head to foot, and its back turned towards her. Absolutely still. Terror transfixed Rachel' (42). The episode is frightening, but her eventual relief that the woman is no ghost is short-lived. In fact, something far worse has been reserved for her. The story derives its considerable impact from the conflict between expectation and actuality. When the ghost does finally materialize, Rachel is not alone as she had assumed she would be, but surrounded by the concert audience, and the ghost appears in a form she had not anticipated:

> And then it seemed that the moth itself, the solid black shape, became as big as its shadow, and the shadow grew many times bigger. Big as a person ... Suddenly, it was hovering right in front of Rachel's face. Black, black like a robe, with a little bit of white and paleness on top. (43)

This is frightening, but then the violent hand of her father intrudes:

> Then Dad's arm crashed across, with his open tweed cap in his fist. It hit the black thing a terrible sideways blow, and flung it into the heart of the roaring flames in the great Gothic fireplace. There it hovered a moment, still fluttering to live. Then there was a puff of dark grey smoke, and a slight and evil smell, and it was quite gone. (43)

What Rachel had not anticipated was that she would feel, not fear, but pity: '"But didn't you *see*," she shouted. "It had a human face! It wanted me to help her. Didn't you *see*?"' (44). In this story, Westall extends his persistent request for sympathy into the realm of the supernatural: it is not only the living who need our sympathy, so too do the dead.

The young male narrator of 'Sea Coal' is on a Job Creation scheme, which he loathes, as much for the ignorance of his co-workers as for the pointless banality of the job itself. After a fight, he prevents the others from drowning a cat and as he walks away, he says: 'I just hated the whole of bloody 1982 and I wished to hell I was somewhere else, anywhere ... So I never really grasped how I got out o' the far side o' the wood and into that slum' (92–3). He finds himself in 1932. Like 'The Bus', 'Sea Coal' is both 'time slip' story and wish-fulfilment narrative. Inevitably, what the narrator learns is how fortunate he is to live in 1982. In 1932 he sees poverty, disease, unemployment unalleviated by social security cheques, and despair. In addition, he also sees on the beach, where he searches for the sea coal of the title, a radically polarized society: 'The beach was cut in half, as if by a knife. The sunny, southern half was full of holidaymakers in deckchairs. On the cold, northern end of the beach, shadowed by the cliffs ... crawled a grey stooping army of old women, thin coughing men and little kids. Each with their soaking black bag' (101).

'Sea Coal' is a muted critique, not only of the poverty of the past, but of a generation unaware of its considerable privileges. When the narrator attempts to persuade the tubercular Manny to come to 1982 with him, the following exchange takes place: ' "C'mon, Manny," I said. "You must try. Not much further. There's doctors can make you well over there, Manny. Plenty o' food – nobody goes hungry." "Sounds like the bleddy kingdom o' heaven," said Manny, and began coughing again' (103).

Westall is too level-headed to offer the present as anything like 'the kingdom of heaven', but he is bold enough to use 'time slip' narratives like 'Sea Coal' to teach his young readers that without a historical context it is difficult to appreciate the huge gains that have been made in social welfare over the past fifty years.

Characteristically, it is the cat which permits the narrator to slip from one era into another, and both 'A Walk on the Wild Side' and 'Creatures in the House' are supernatural stories at the centre of which are cats. In 'A Walk on the Wild Side' the narrator immediately establishes the duality of cats: 'Two natures. A purring bundle in your arms; a contemplative Buddha by the fire. But those pointed ears are moving even in sleep, listening to the windy dark outside' (130). The male narrator, a fifty-year-old school teacher, describes the way in which the mysterious female kitten Rama comes into his life. He also notes: 'For all her poor beginning, Rama grew amazingly fast' (131). As has been seen in several of Westall's other stories, accelerated development, in animals or humans, is always a sign of the uncanny, and so it proves here. Rama eventually takes the form of a woman, manifesting herself to the narrator as seductive, cruel, and, ultimately, murderous.

'A Walk on the Wild Side' is a displacement narrative, using the cat to construct a story which is really concerned with establishing the dual nature of women, not cats. The first person narration renders this less a universal statement, inseparable from the omniscient narrative perspective, and more one which is idiosyncratic, unique to a lonely 50-year-old man. It is a provocative, cleverly-told tale, generating fear in the reader perhaps not as much for the story itself as the manner in which it slips easily between realism, dreams, and the supernatural, removing any sense of certainty.

'Creatures in the House' is perhaps the best story in the collection. Sally Walmsley inherits her aunt's house, on condition she lives in it. A creature lives inside the house, a parasite which has slowly taken the life of her aunt and which has forced her to shift Sally in as a replacement before she dies: 'It only liked women, yet would have found a brisk WI meeting an unbearable hell. It fed on women alone; women in despair' (72). Sally herself is desperately unhappy, having been abandoned by her married lover. The parasite begins to prey on her, just as it did her aunt, and her aunt before her. What saves Sally, in an episode reminiscent of a similar incident in *Blitzcat*, is a typical Westall emotion: 'Sally felt a tiny surge of sympathy' (74). It is, of course, a cat for which Sally feels sympathy and she is rewarded for her feelings of pity. The cat brings home other cats, until the house is full of them. Mercilessly, the cats hunt the parasite down, not, Westall implies, because they wish to help Sally but because it is in their nature to hunt and kill.

The story is impressive in a number of ways. Like *Blitzcat* it is remarkably convincing as a cat's eye view of the world: 'The memory of the mince grew to a mountain in his mind; a lovely blood-oozing salty mountain' (79). The title is also of interest; although there is only one parasite, the title refers to 'creatures' in the house, because, of course, the cats too are creatures, and are both parasitical and murderous. Perhaps most impressively of all, Westall is able evoke sympathy for the parasite, as the savage and remorseless cats close in for the kill:

> And confused and bewildered by so many enemies, weak from hunger and shattered by frustration, the creature was cowering up on its shelf, trying to get out into the open air through the thick

brickwork of the chimneys. But it was old, old ... (88)

The year after the publication of this collection Westall published *The Cats of Seroster* (1984), a fantasy set in medieval France, in which cats play as important a role as humans, and have as much dialogue. *The Cats of Seroster* is an interesting generic experiment, and, as always, Westall stresses the almost inhuman cruelty and violence of the past, but both 'A Walk on the Wild Side' and 'Creatures in the House' are considerably more sinister and horrifying. While the novel signals itself consistently as a fantasy, both of the short stories combine comprehensive mimetic details with a fluid, shifting and ontologically treacherous world; one which promises horror and generates fear.

Urn Burial (1987) may well be the apotheosis of Westall's preoccupation with cats, although *The Christmas Cat*, published four years later, in which a cat replaces Jesus in the manger, is an equally strong contender. At the opening of *Urn Burial*, Ralph, a young shepherd, is described as hating the present day, and, unusually for a Westall protagonist, loathing machinery. Westall presumably took the title for *Urn Burial* from Sir Thomas Browne's work of the same name, first published in 1658. Browne's *Urn Burial* is a meditation on burial customs, and in Westall's *Urn Burial*, while Ralph is out tending his flock he discovers a tomb buried in the hills, left behind by an ancient species, the Fefethil, who have obviously come to Earth from outer space and who are engaged in an on-going war with another species, the Wawaka. The Fefethil are actually as close to being cats as is possible. Ralph retrieves the helmet of one of their greatest warriors, Prepoc, and, in effect, 'becomes' a cat, helping the Fefethil to continue and eventually win the war. The novel is reminiscent of *Blitzcat* and 'The Creatures in the House' in its depiction of a cat's-eye view of the world. Generically, it appears to be a straightforward alien novel, and it has elements within it of the wish-fulfilment narrative. Essentially, however, *Urn Burial* is a pastoral, emphasizing its generic status by making Ralph a literal shepherd. Ralph's hatred of machinery and his contempt for the modern age are indicative of a desire which is fundamentally regressive. The novel's drive is prelapsarian; Ralph wishes to return to a more innocent time, to a state of primal innocence. The fears it subliminally addresses are likely to be those associated with the adolescent's anxieties about becoming an adult.

Urn Burial is, for Westall, an unusually didactic novel, and uses a series of alien perspectives to offer overt criticisms of vivisection, fox hunting, and cruelty to animals in general. The novel also takes a particular satisfaction in criticizing humanity's history of gleefully murdering one another. The Fefethil call humans 'apes', as a mark of contempt for their uncivilized state, and an interesting exchange takes place between Theloc, a Fefethil elder, and Ralph: ' "You are no fool, for an ape." "Me? I'm dead thick. I've only got two O levels." "You have a sympathy with other animals, other races, your ape-scientists will never have" ' (102).

Ralph's ability to feel sympathy decisively marks him out, no matter how furry or bewhiskered the context, as a typical Westall protagonist.

In 1989 Westall published another important collection of short stories: *Ghosts and Journeys*. Four of the stories are supernatural tales, and of these, two are ghost stories. 'The Borgia Mirror', however, is a 'time slip' narrative, although unusually, the shifts in time must be deduced by the reader, and they are not experienced by the protagonist. As often happens in Westall's fiction, particularly in the later work, an historical object is invested with the character traits of its most famous owner. 'The Borgia Mirror' is as cheerfully amoral as anything by Roald Dahl, and neatly conflates Westall's preoccupation with antiques and time travel.

'The Boys' Toilets' is a finely-judged ghost story, at the centre of which is the concept of justified retribution. As occurs in 'Blackham's Wimpey', the ghost in 'The Boys' Toilets' has a legitimate grievance, and indeed it is rare for a ghost in Westall's work to return to the world of the living arbitrarily. It is an important aspect of the story that a girls' school should move into a empty boys' school and that it is in the boys' toilets that the girls become aware that there is the ghost of a boy haunting the toilets. 'The Boys' Toilets' also suggests that the amiable and well-meaning vicar and father of the protagonist, Rebeccah, is powerless against the forces of the supernatural. As he does so impressively in *The Watch House*, Westall describes the inorganic world in similes which serve to merge the living with the dead: 'She stood paralysed, staring at the teethlike ranks of the tombstones that grinned at her in the faintest light of the last street-lamp' (39). 'Rosalie' is another ghost story set in a school and, again, the protagonist, Jane, is a girl, but this time the ghost, the eponymous Rosalie, is also a girl. Here, the haunting is, strikingly, unjustified. Jane's uncle, Geoff, is himself a writer of ghost stories and 'Rosalie' has an intriguing metafictional aspect, as Uncle Geoff attempts to deny the actuality of a real ghost by constructing for Jane an imaginary ghost story more powerful than the ghost of Rosalie. Significantly, he fails, and Rosalie's ghost destroys the entire school. Both 'The Boys' Toilets' and 'Rosalie' stress the inability of middle-aged men to grasp the reality of the world of the supernatural as apprehended by two sensitive, adolescent girls.

'The Journey', the final story in the collection, is truly remarkable; a Beckettian evocation of a nightmarish, transitional state between life and death. The story's protagonist, Ted, is male, and has been injured in a motor-cycle accident. He seems to wake up in horrifying circumstances:

> Ted wakened in total blackness.
> And total silence.
> He tried to shout. Nothing came. Not even a whimper.
> He felt for his mouth, to see why it didn't work.
> No mouth, no hands, no body at all. Only the memory of having had body, mouth, hands.
> Terror filled him like ice. He started to scream. And couldn't. He realized for the first time what a privilege it had been to scream, whimper, hide his face in his hands. He couldn't do any of it. (147)

Ted begins to understand that this hideous place is populated by evil creatures he dubs 'The Eaters', who consume the souls of the weak and the frightened. Like the scarecrows in Westall's earlier novel, the Eaters are animated by hate. Ted allies himself with the spirits of the many dogs who inhabit the place, and together they search for people who can be saved. Westall's characteristic attitude to the female is clearly in evidence here. The most powerful of his canine allies is Zero: 'A pack was forming. Sometimes they had to stop for a long time, in a whirl of confusion, while the pack-order was sorted out. But always Zero remained on top, a merciful and motherly leader, a typical bitch' (152). 'The Journey' is a strikingly powerful story, ultimately optimistic, but harrowing none the less. Again, Westall's powerful similes drive his narrative forward:

> The plea for help shot through the bubble like a knife. The pleading was human, female. 'Oh, no, no, no, noooooh.' Each 'no' was like a desperate fist, beating helplessly against a second worse dying; like the sicking-up of a fact too horrible to stay in the mind. (153)

The story strikes an interesting balance between the two concepts of Christianity and Humanism. Initially, Ted's prayers help him to resist the Eaters, but as the story progresses it is clearly suggested that it is his altruism and sympathy for the defenceless which returns him to life. With 'Blackham's Wimpey' and 'The Stones of Muncaster Cathedral', 'The Journey' is one of Westall's finest, and most horrifying, short stories.

Strictly speaking, Westall's 1989 collection *Echoes of War* contains no horror stories. However, 'The Making of Me' is an interesting first-person account of the way a grandfather passes on his love for historical objects to his grandson, thereby merging two of Westall's most ubiquitous subjects. In fact, a third characteristic preoccupation of Westall's is also found within the story: time travel, although here it is represented as occurring without supernatural agency. The passion the narrator feels for historical objects is rooted in a desire which links 'The Making of Me' to *Urn Burial*: 'All part of my journey back in time. The world goes forward to drugs and violence and fruit-machine addiction. I go backwards to where I am truly free' (89). 'After the Funeral' is a supernatural 'time slip' narrative but, on this occasion, one of the time travellers learns less about the cruelty of the past than he does about his own cruelty. It is a colloquially-told story, in the first person, and the narrator describes a night when flying a commercial aircraft to Germany from England the aircraft slips back to 1942. The narrator's first officer, Stringer, has just told him that his father's funeral had been the previous day, and that his father had shot himself. Stringer tells the narrator that his father had been in the RAF during World War II, but had been unable to hold down a job for years after the war. Stringer is savage about his father's depression, lethargy, and rages, and ends his summary of his father's character even more cruelly: 'A pointless bloody life,' said Stringer, 'and a pointless bloody death. Pity he didn't do it years ago, then my mother could've found somebody nicer' (41). It is at this moment that the aircraft emerges from the clouds and the crew find themselves in 1942, experiencing all the horrors of war in the air. Eventually, Stringer breaks down: 'He just sat there in his seat, tears streaming down his face, saying over and over again, "Sorry, Dad. Sorry, sorry, sorry. I just didn't understand"' (52). The narrator remains unaware of the harsh and salutary lesson which Stringer has received, but the reader is left in no doubt that Stringer has learned, too late to understand or help his father, the importance of sympathy.

In the same year that *Echoes of War* (1989) appeared, Westall published another collection: *The Call and Other Stories*. In the first story, 'Woman and Home', a boy who is being bullied at school plays truant and finds himself in an abandoned house, haunted by the ghost of a Miss Nadine Marriner. The boy realizes that her ghost has already murdered several others who have been in the house before him, but he is allowed to escape, primarily because unlike his predecessors, who see only the financial value of objects, he is aesthetically enchanted by a beautiful clock. The story anticipates the adventure novel *A Place*

For Me, where the heroine's life is saved because she will not sell a lovely clock. As noted earlier, Westall's preoccupations are not confined to specific genres; a clock, for example, is just as likely to be central to an adventure novel as it is to a ghost story. The last story in the collection, 'The Red House Clock', also centres around a specific clock, but the story contains several rhapsodies on the beauty of clocks in general:

> But my great love was clocks. Nothing lives like a clock. Nothing can be your friend on a lonely dark evening like a clock ... I loved nothing better than to discover a clock in a house we were selling-up. In some cupboard, long-abandoned. Thick with cobwebs as a haunted house; blistered all down one side by the sun; stained white with the creeping blight of damp. Clocks like little houses, little haunted churches, little ruined black temples, from which all life had gone and only memory remained. And I would say, like Jesus said of the widow's son, 'He is not dead, but sleepeth.' And set to work. (102)

The story powerfully stresses Westall's persistent suggestion that the spirit of the dead can reside in objects; it is an intriguingly primitive idea, blurring magic and the supernatural, and it is strikingly at odds with the scientific rationalism of contemporary culture.

'Uncle Otto at Denswick Park' is a comic, 'time slip' story, and 'Warren, Sharon and Darren' is a rather moving alien narrative, clearly indebted to Steven Spielberg's film *ET: The Extra-terrestrial*. Darren provides another example of unnaturally accelerated development indicating the presence of the uncanny, and it soon becomes apparent that the child is an alien and that he has awesome powers. At the conclusion of the story, as the other aliens come back to claim Darren, he tells Sharon why they chose her to be his mother: ' "they are ... cold, cold. They had forgotten how to ... *feel*. You ... taught me to feel" ' (61). As in *Urn Burial*, the aliens single out a human being who is not intellectual, but sympathetic. It is safe to assume that many adolescent readers, unsure of their own intellectual abilities, but convinced of their emotional adequacy, respond favourably to narratives such as these, which, in effect, give precedence to emotion over intellect.

'The Badger' is an extremely clever story, told in the form of a police report. This report recounts the circumstances that have led to the deaths of two men, killed by James Long, a notorious badger-digger, who sells the badgers for fighting. The precise and logical policeman is forced to use the linguistic register of his profession to convey Long's belief that he is being haunted by the ghost of a giant badger come to seek revenge. What could have been a preposterous story is actually extremely impressive, primarily because of the narrative tension generated between Long's obvious belief that he is being haunted, and the scepticism of the policeman who is reporting his story. A practical explanation for the 'haunting' is also offered, and it is clearly the one which the policeman prefers, but the alternative ghost story is never displaced by this explanation: the two co-exist as equal possibilities. It is certainly possible that such ambivalence as this is Westall's overarching goal.

The title story of the collection, 'The Call', clearly has its origins in Westall's own experiences as a Samaritan. There are few people who understand fear better than Samaritans. The story uses a first-person narrator to frame what is essentially an omniscient narrative. Generically it is both an extremely sinister ghost story, and a 'time slip' narrative. The married couple on Samaritan duty on Christmas Eve receive a series of phone calls from a woman, Agnes Todd, claiming that her husband is about to kill her. She plays the couple off against one another, eventually enticing the wife out to her cottage, by the river. Her husband, meanwhile, has realized that Agnes is a ghost and arrives just in time to stop his wife, who is in a trance, from joining Agnes in the freezing water. The story's coda, which takes place at the funeral of Harry Lancaster, an ex-director of this branch of the Samaritans, makes it clear that Harry had worked alone on Christmas Eve for several decades because he knew Agnes would call: ' "So he talked to her all those years … knowing?" "Aye, but he wouldn't let anybody else do Christmas Eve. She was lonely, but he knew she was dangerous. Lonely an' dangerous. She wanted company" ' (93).

Agnes Todd's surname means 'death' in German, and also alludes to the expression 'on your tod', meaning 'on your own'. It is absolutely characteristic of Westall's fiction that her ghost, although committed to luring the living to their deaths, should be spoken of sympathetically.

The Stones of Muncaster Cathedral (1991) contains only two long stories: the title story and 'Brangwyn Gardens'. The latter story, set in 1955, is the account of an elaborate hoax played upon a young male student by an older woman. Using a diary set in 1945, the story shifts between the two periods, but, due to the nature of the hoax itself, 1945 and 1955 become disconcertingly and disturbingly intertwined. As always, Westall's depiction of civilian life during World War II evokes the danger and the privations of the period, and the courage of people under appalling conditions. Just like his supernatural 'time slip' narratives, 'Brangwyn Gardens' also stresses the horrors of the past, and throws into relief the security and plenitude of the present. However, it is worth noting that in the absence of physical danger, the story's protagonist becomes susceptible to supernatural fears. The protagonist's sensations of anxiety and fear at what he assumes is a ghost segue into an equally fearful realization that his landlady is insane. As so often occurs in Westall's work, fear is both supernatural and pragmatic in origin. Overall, Westall's writing about the war, from both the civilian and the military perspectives, is enthralling and evocative, and yet also informative and provocative. It gives pleasure, while it teaches.

'The Stones of Muncaster Cathedral' won the Dracula Society's Children of the Night Award and certainly it is among Westall's finest supernatural stories. It is written in the retrospective, first person, and relies heavily on a series of anticipatory observations only made possible by its retrospection: 'Then I told myself it was just stone, and the work of men's hands and the wind and the frost, and not to be so bloody stupid. Anyway, that's what I told myself at the time' (13). It was suggested earlier that 'The Journey' was 'Beckettian'; in much the same way 'The Stones of Muncaster Cathedral' seems indebted to William Golding's 1964 novel *The Spire*. Central to both texts is the conflict between a rational stonemason and a priest who is convinced of the reality of supernatural forces. A striking difference between the two, however, is that while there is a simple polarity between good and evil in Westall's story, *The Spire* is theologically more sophisticated, suggesting that good and evil are so intertwined that it is impossible to separate them. In 'The Stones of Muncaster Cathedral' it is evil which demands human sacrifice, but in *The Spire*, Golding boldly suggests that it may equally well be God. In *The Spire*, the stonemason dies a sceptic, but in Westall's story the stonemason lives to learn that a baleful force we call 'evil' still exists in the world. Again, like so many of Westall's male protagonists, Joe Clarke learns of the limitations inherent in rationalism.

Joe is given the job of repairing the south-west tower of Muncaster Cathedral. As soon as he looks at the tower he sees the gargoyles, and one in particular. Initially he is professionally pragmatic: 'They never worried me; just honest stone and the work of men's hands, and the work of wind and rain. But this one; it really looked as if it was watching me' (12). By the story's conclusion, however, he has learnt, again like many of Westall's protagonists, that historical objects can be animated by evil spirits. As the story progresses, the cathedral's evil emanations extend beyond the church grounds and begin to send young children into somnambulistic states prior to luring them to their deaths. Joe manages to save his own son, but at this point he ceases to be a committed rationalist. His co-worker and friend is killed in an 'accident', and with the help of a local policeman, Hughie Allardyce, Joe discovers the horror that is, literally, at the centre of the cathedral:

> 'A ... skull,' said Hughie Allardyce. 'A little child's ... skull' ... But I looked further. There was more than a skull; there was a whole tiny skeleton wedged down into the narrow slot, still sitting with its knees forced up near its head, and its arms folded in between. And down below, the grey shining strands grew thicker and thicker through the bones, tying the tiny form to the stone. (88)

Joe tells Allardyce what he thinks has happened: ' "I reckon it's taking the goodness out of the child, feeding it into ... the stone. All these years" ' (89). At the discovery of its terrible secret, the tower collapses, and Joe confesses that he only managed to escape certain death because a 'voice', which he clearly apprehends as spiritual, told him to move his head. In a nice twist, however, the vicar gives up religion to become a social worker.

'The Stones of Muncaster Cathedral' is unusual for Westall in its emphasis upon the horror of an individual's crimes, rather than on the cruelty and violence of an entire historical period. The story is characteristic of Westall's work in general, however, in its use of the policeman. The police, as can be seen in this story, in 'The Badger', 'A Walk on the Wild Side', *Urn Burial*, and 'Sergeant Nice', have the same function as several senior airforce officers in *Blitzcat*, 'Blackham's Wimpey', and 'After the Funeral', and the same role to play as the Samaritan's Duty Officer in 'The Call': they represent the impossibility of translating the rhetoric of the supernatural into language appropriate for the official forms so necessary for the efficient running of a contemporary, rational society. In her introduction to this book Kim Reynolds refers to the *X-Files*, noting that the series revolves around a number of assumptions: 'all governments are duplicitous, power structures deliberately obscure, the media corrupt, and most people and relationships untrustworthy.' In addition, it can be noted that typically an episode will conclude with Scully unable to use an official FBI report to describe the paranormal events that she and Mulder have recently experienced. As Allardyce says to Joe at the conclusion of 'The Stones of Muncaster Cathedral': 'Between you and me ... Half the stuff that happens in the world goes into reports, and half doesn't. And it's the important part that doesn't' (97).

Yaxley's Cat (1991), as its title suggests, and like so much of Westall's fiction, places a cat at the centre of the narrative. It is similar to 'Brangwyn Gardens' in that an ostensibly supernatural occurrence is revealed to be human in origin, and it also uses the same anticipatory narrative technique to generate fear and anxiety in the reader as 'The Stones of Muncaster Cathedral'. The omniscient narrator, for example, notes of the family in *Yaxley's Cat*: 'It was their last happy evening' (43). In *Yaxley's Cat* Rose and her two children rent an abandoned cottage in a small, rural village. They discover that the previous inhabitant of the cottage, the Yaxley of the title, who has mysteriously disappeared, was a 'Cunning Man', a healer, and, so it was believed in the village, a man with supernatural powers. Eventually, Rose and the children discover that Yaxley was murdered by the villagers and buried in his own garden.

The novel is similar to *The Wind Eye* in its depiction of Rose's husband, Philip, off-stage for the entire novel, who, like Bertrand, is a practical, rational man. Again, as occurs in *The Wind Eye*, the fearful aspects of Christianity are stressed: 'It had never occurred to her before that angels like Michael and Gabriel could be a bit scary. But after all, they had to put down devils, trample them under their feet ... ' (89). It is observations such as these, rather than the similar setting of a story in a cathedral, that bring Westall closer to Golding's view that good and evil are inseparable. The novel, inevitably, has virtually the whole village threatening Rose and the children, establishing a dichotomy which revolves, not around the supernatural and the rational as is first supposed, but around the rural and the urban, and, ultimately, around violence and the law. Perhaps the most striking feature of the novel is the way in which Rose and her children provide a more complex, internal dichotomy than the one established by the family's opposition to the villagers.

The novel begins with the children rejecting Rose's old-fashioned fairy stories; instead, they learn about witches, knowledge which becomes extremely useful to them, from watching television. In the course of the novel, Rose becomes disturbed at the cynicism, pragmatism, and even violence of her own children. In *Yaxley's Cat*, for the first time in one of Westall's fictions, the value of empathy is interrogated. While waiting for the villagers to storm the cottage and kill them, and listening to the cunning violence of her children's strategies, Rose remembers hearing a soldier on the radio saying that young people make the best killers because they have no imagination; they cannot understand what it is to inflict or suffer pain and death: 'Mature people make the worst killers, the colonel had said. Because they can empathize with pain. My God, she thought, I am a useless quivering mass of empathy' (126). Rose candidly accepts at the novel's conclusion that without her children's pragmatism and violence she, and they, would be dead, but she is deeply troubled nonetheless. The novel ends with the restoration of law and order over anarchy and murder, but it is a far from triumphalist conclusion. The vicar, who has been quite prepared throughout the narrative to accept supernatural explanations, comes over to comfort her, but Rose's last words are despairing: ' "Oh, vicar," she said. "Is there no mercy anywhere?" ' (137). The vicar tells her that there is, but, significantly, he suggests that this mercy is not found in God, but in one of Rose's neighbours and in Rose herself. As occurs in 'The Journey', the possibility of religious consolation becomes attenuated throughout the narrative and is replaced by the more pragmatic consolations offered by Humanism. Placed against this, and generating a tension which is unreconciled at the novel's conclusion, is Westall's suggestion, made near the end of his writing career, and indeed near the end of his life, that empathy, far from being empowering, may well be debilitating.

Gulf (1992) was shortlisted for the Whitbread Award. Generically *Gulf* is like much of Westall's work, combining elements of two genres; in this case, the war story and the supernatural novel. The novel is in the first person, again heavily reliant on the anticipatory narrative techniques that characterize Westall's later fiction: 'That was the last time I was to feel better; 'til the end' (71). Such observations slowly build up fear and suspense in the reader. Throughout the novel, it is implied that the 'end' will be death, but this is not the case, at least, not quite. The narrator, Tom, tells the story of his brother, Andy, also known in the family as Figgis, who has telepathic gifts which are principally generated by his empathy with the worlds' victims. Tom, initially, has no such empathy, and a crucial aspect of the novel is the characteristic movement from ignorance to sympathy. Tom says to his father of the starving in Africa, the flood victims of Bangladesh: ' "They breed like rabbits, and then they can't feed themselves. If they were birds or foxes dying, people would just call it the balance of nature. Two-thirds of the birds and foxes born every year die of starvation. But when it's people … any people … " ' (25). By the novel's conclusion, he has, of course, learnt sympathy.

Just before the beginning of the Gulf War, Figgis starts talking in his sleep, calling himself 'Latif', and speaking Arabic. 'Latif' gradually starts to take Figgis over, and Tom begins to understand that in some mysterious way Figgis has become another boy, a boy in the Gulf. As the Gulf War progresses, Figgis's situation becomes desperate and it seems inevitable that when the Americans kill Latif, Figgis will also die. *Gulf* constitutes a return to convention for Westall, after the interrogation of empathy in *Yaxley's Cat*. In *Gulf* empathy is clearly desirable, and while in the earlier novel television is capable of imparting useful information, one of *Gulf*'s primary concerns is to depict the reality of war as opposed to the sanitized television sound bites which masquerade as 'coverage'. Dr Rashid, the psychiatrist called in to help Figgis and himself from the Middle East, joins a long list of Westall's officials who find themselves unable to translate supernatural events into a language acceptable to a rational society: ' "If I wrote these things in my case notes, I would be struck off as a lunatic myself. Yet it is so, I cannot deny it" ' (74).

Ingeniously *Gulf* only pretends to trick the reader. At the novel's conclusion, Figgis, in effect, does die, justifying the rhetoric of mourning which drives the narrative, but Andy lives, having completely lost the empathy that made him become Latif. Tom, however, mourns the loss of his gentle brother, and has learnt lifelong lessons from the experience.

Demons and Shadows (1993, US; 1998 UK) is a collection of Westall's supernatural stories, several of which have been considered earlier in this chapter. 'The Last Day of Miss Dorinda Molyneaux' is a very clever and impressively atmospheric ghost story, which uses its title to raise expectations about its conclusion which are unfulfilled. In this story, it is not the male narrator who undergoes change, but the eponymous Dorinda. After a terrifying encounter in the crypt of a church with a ghost, the narrator says of her: 'But it wasn't the Dorinda Molyneaux I'd known. The unshakable confidence had gone; the certainty that there was a practical answer for everything' (257). Typically, a policeman is unable to explain supernatural events to his superiors, and the narrator notes: 'There are some things that are best not entered in policemen's notebooks, if only for the sake of Chief Constables and the judiciary' (256).

'Graveyard Shift', as the punning title implies, is a ghost story which manages to be both comic and sinister. It involves child abuse and vampirism, but with the exception of 'St Austell Friars', Westall seems never to have regarded vampires seriously as agents of horror. 'The Death of Wizards' is, in essence, a fairy story, and combines several of Westall's preoccupations, notably the elderly, time travel, and antiques. It is also a wish-fulfilment narrative, and, inevitably, the protagonist regrets having his wish fulfilled. 'The Woolworth Spectacles' is, again, a characteristic Westall story, concerned with the arcane way in which an historical object is capable of transmitting the personality of a previous owner into the new owner. 'Rachel and the Angel' is also a wish-fulfilment story. Rachel, who is lonely and bored, enters her father's church:

> Dullness. Five hundred years of dullness. She could've screamed.
> If only something wonderful or terrible would happen, just once.
> Instead of dusty wooden angels, a real angel, like in the Bible ...
> In that instant, though she'd heard no one come in, she knew she
> was no longer alone in the church. (7)

It is worth noting that many of Westall's most powerful stories take a church, or an abbey, or a cathedral as their *locus*, in sharp distinction to Point Horror narratives, in which churches simply do not exist.

'A Nose Against the Glass' is a virtual compendium of Westall's characteristic concerns. It is set for the most part in an antique shop, but culminates in a church, and is concerned throughout with cats, Christmas, and the elderly. The aged protagonist, with the symbolic name of Widdowson, has become covetous and uncharitable. He sees a child outside his shop whom he assumes is Christ, and runs after him into a church, where he dies. Before he dies he manages to scribble a note, leaving all his money to children. In a brilliantly realistic coda, however, the reader is informed: 'The will he left in the church was not granted probate, lacking any witnesses that he was "of sound testamentary disposition". His earlier will prevailed' (163). 'A Nose Against the Glass' is a religious fable, reminiscent of Oscar Wilde's 'The Selfish Giant'. It offers a characteristic change of heart, which the logical and judicial procedures of society deny. *The Wheatstone Pond* (1993), published the year of Westall's death, is a strikingly sinister, supernatural novel. The first person narrator is a slightly shady antiques dealer whose shop is near the Wheatstone Pond, in which seven people have committed suicide in five years. The authorities decide to drain the pond and a number of old objects are retrieved, several of which, the narrator discovers, are linked to a number of abominable crimes. Although *The Wheatstone Pond* seems to offer a simple conflict between good and evil, it resembles *Yaxley's Cat* in that the narrative is complicated by the internal conflict between the narrator and his assistant, James, a Methodist lay preacher. The narrator is, initially, a rational man, ill-disposed to accept supernatural explanations, but James, correctly of course, attributes the evil of the Wheatstone Pond and the old abbey connected with it, to supernatural evil. The novel's heroine, Hermione, is also convinced of the existence of supernatural evil, and of the efficacy of prayer:

' "I pray very seldom, and very badly. But I have known prayers answered. And when you've got something very big and very nasty and very mysterious against you, it's a comfort to have something very big and very nice and very mysterious on your side" ' (123).

By the novel's conclusion, inevitably, the narrator has been forced to learn that rationalism is too limited a perspective to make sense of a world which can be mysterious, irrational, and frightening beyond belief.

Robert Westall's supernatural fiction is among the most powerful writing for young people published in the second half of last century. It is not difficult to imagine an adolescent reader experiencing a number of the responses that Twitchell lists at the beginning of this chapter: tension, shuddering, recoiling, chilling, etc. while reading Westall's work. Most strikingly Westall's work evokes sensations of fear in the reader, particularly in fiction like 'Blackham's Wimpey', *The Wheatstone Pond*, 'The Stones of Muncaster Cathedral', 'The Call', and dozens of other of Westall's stories and novels. Perhaps, however, what is most impressive about Westall's fiction is the way in which the evocation of fear complements the addressing of fear. A novel such as *The Scarecrows*, for example, generates fear by its ominous ghosts and their diet of hate, and it addresses fear by using the ghost story to raise emotional anxieties about death, grief, and mourning. This duality is itself complemented by the artful manner in which two different types of reality often interpenetrate one another; the creation of such ontological confusion creates fears in the reader which might be considered useful, in that they invite the questioning of the nature of reality. Enthralling, thoughtful, evocative, and profoundly moral, Westall's work emphasizes the link that should exist between generations, the inability of rationalism to thoroughly explain a mysterious universe, the connections individuals must make with the larger community, and, perhaps most importantly, the inevitability, and appropriateness of old age and death.

Books by Robert Westall

Blitz
Blitzcat
Blizzard
Break of Dark
The Call and Other Stories
The Cats of Seroster

The Christmas Cat
The Christmas Ghost
Christmas Spirit
The Creature in the Dark
Demons and Shadows
The Devil on the Road
Echoes of War
Falling into Glory
Fathom Five
Fearful Lovers
Futuretrack Five
Ghost Abbey
Ghosts and Journeys
Gulf
Harvest
The Haunting of Chas McGill
If Cats Could Fly
The Kingdom By the Sea
Love Match
The Machine-Gunners
The Night Mare
Old Man on a Horse
A Place for Me
The Promise
Rachel and the Angel
The Scarecrows
Shades of Darkness
Size Twelve
The Stones of Muncaster Cathedral
Stormsearch
A Time of Fire
Urn Burial
Voices in the Wind
A Walk on the Wild Side
The Watch House
The Wheatstone Pond
The Wind Eye
The Witness
Yaxley's Cat

Anthologies
Cats' Whispers and Tales
Ghost Stories

Non-fiction
Children of the Blitz

Websites
The following sites are likely to be of interest to readers of Westall's fiction:

Tynemouth Pictures
Photographic scenes of this coastal town in the north-east. http://www.fgillings.freeserve.co.uk/homepage.htm
(Webcrawler)

Robert Westall Trail
http://www.readingnorth.org.uk/westall.htm (*AltaVista*)

Guided Tour Dates 2000
http://www.readingnorth.org.uk/tours.htm (*Infoseek*)

Robert Westall
http://www.norham.n-tyneside.sch.uk/westall/index.htm (*AltaVista*)

Notes
1 N. Carroll (1990) *The Philosophy of Horror*. London: Routledge, p. 24.
2 Tony Magistral and Michael Morrison (eds) (1996) *A Dark Night's Dreaming: Contemporary American Horror Fiction*. Columbia, South Carolina: University of South Carolina Press, p. 2.
3 Carroll, *op. cit.*, p. 199.
4 S. King (1991) *Danse Macabre*. London: Futura, p. 48.
5 http://www.norham.n-tyneside.sch.uk/westall/index.htm, 14/04/00.

CHAPTER 3

The Game Called Death: Frightening Fictions by David Almond, Philip Gross and Lesley Howarth

Geraldine Brennan

Which is more frightening, the attic or the cellar? Would you rather hide in the shed with the spiders or behind the curtains where you can't breathe and your toe might stick out so that your appalling cousin will find you as surely as Jane Eyre's did? When he does, would you rather be tickled to death, flayed with elastic bands or shut back in the shed?

Many readers experienced their first horror narratives as home movies directed by the biggest or nastiest child at the party (or the child with the biggest or nastiest parent) while the grown-ups mercilessly looked the other way. Outdoor locations included the smelly burnt-out car, the prickly hedge and the building site with the huge Alsatian. Games provide early experiences of betrayal, deception, abuse of goodwill and other social evils: games controlled by other children, that is. Playing with other children can be the greatest terror life can hold, except having to play by oneself.

Games also offer a framework for measuring ourselves against unspeakable challenges and trying out identities that we dare not adopt in life. They provide a safe, time-limited structure for accessing and challenging fears. Under the wrong control, they can be humiliating, divisive and cruel. The extremes of experience generated by structured children's play, its swift changes in fortune and its power dynamics, makes it ideal material for a genre in which demands for a resolute pace and the frisson of unpredictability must be met alongside steady progress towards a partly pre-ordained conclusion (in 'the game called Death' in David Almond's second children's novel, *Kit's Wilderness*, which I shall go on to discuss below, the participants know most of what is in store for the 'dead' player and this knowledge adds value to the hidden factors of 'who?' and 'how long?').

The works considered here are David Almond's three novels (*Skellig*, *Kit's Wilderness* and *Heaven Eyes*), *Transformer* and *Facetaker* by Philip Gross, and *Paulina* by Lesley Howarth. All were published in the last five years of the twentieth century, and most since the beginning of 1998. They represent a sample of recent writing which would appeal to young readers in the 12-plus age group (younger for David Almond's books) who enjoy horror series fiction, although only Gross's books appear in an established horror series. The authors have all, to some extent, employed games, rituals and diversions as ways in which their characters can tackle fear of death, loss, or displacement, build their identities and preserve them intact, and, in some cases, influence others for their own ends. The key factor that these books have in common, however, is their empathy with their young protagonists and the immediacy and clarity of their first-person narrative voices.

David Almond's novels are from the 'crossover' stable of literary fiction which is read by both children and adults. While his books are not marketed as horror fiction, Almond engages with the fears of both child and adult protagonists and charts their efforts to resolve them. In each of the three novels a young person must embark on a difficult psychic journey, sustained by the sense of place and history offered by Almond's fictional territory, the north-east of England, and, to a greater or lesser extent, by family and community. The development of this theme can be traced between the three consecutive novels, with John Askew's 'game called Death' at the centre of the middle book, *Kit's Wilderness*, and hence at the heart of Almond's inner literary landscape.

The two novels by Philip Gross, a writer of poetry and fiction for teenagers including the science fiction novel, *Psylicon Beach*, have been selected from the Point Horror Unleashed list, which offers longer and more complex horror series fiction than the original Point Horror series. Gross depicts believable contemporary adolescents with everyday fears about not being cool, not being accepted, not being good enough and (the ultimate fear) ending up like their parents. He shows how their insecurities make them vulnerable to exploitation by unstable or predatory 'gamemaster' figures who seek to recruit groups of acolytes to bolster their egos and achieve their desired outcomes. Once the game plans are in position, Gross's stories move at a frenetic pace.

Lesley Howarth is a versatile and prolific writer of fiction for children of all ages, most acclaimed for the sophisticated novels published throughout the 1990s for readers aged around 11 and above, such as *MapHead*, *Maphead2*, *Weather Eye* and *The Flower King*. Her books are hard to categorize, but often weave concerns such as the displacement felt by aliens and the potential of the Internet (which she anticipated in *Weather Eye* in 1995) into wide-ranging narratives with big ideas about society and the future. *Paulina*, a polished, self-contained and psychologically gruelling horror story which looks within rather than without, represents the latest departure for Howarth. The self-assured and appealing narrator is shaken by the two weeks her family spends in New England in a holiday home that comes with a sitting tenant: a 14-year-old girl who died in the basement and plays her games alone.

'Kids' games, eh? What they like?' (*Kit's Wilderness*, 21)

David Almond is one of a handful of writers who made a sudden and dramatic contribution to literature for young people towards the end of the twentieth century. The appearance in 1998 of his first published novel, *Skellig*, followed twenty years' work as a writer of short stories for adults, including six years as editor of the fiction magazine *Panurge*. The tale of Michael, his friend Mina and the angel figure whom Michael finds living in his garage was his first work for children – 'an audience whose minds are fluid, able to accept all kinds of possibilities', Almond states in his introduction to a collection by the winners of The Arts Council Writers' Award 2000.[1] *Skellig* won an Arts Council Award, and also the Carnegie Medal and the Whitbread Children's Book of the Year award. His two following novels for children, *Kit's Wilderness* (1999) and *Heaven Eyes* (2000) have also met with critical acclaim, and *Kit's Wilderness* was on the shortlist for the 1999 Carnegie Medal.

These novels have been earmarked by critics as likely to appeal to both child and adult readerships. 'These dark, poetic children's books are finding a crossover audience' according to S. F. Said in *The Daily Telegraph*[2]. In an article about the renaissance currently being enjoyed by books for children which look beyond the child's immediate experience in society, Said quotes Philip Pullman, a more established writer for children with a crossover readership for his fantasy trilogy, *His Dark Materials*:

> At the best-selling end, adult literature is about childish things: does my bum look big in this? Will Arsenal win the Cup? But children's literature is about grown-up things. Where did we

come from? Where do we go? What is consciousness?

Said points out that Pullman's trilogy 'revolves around fundamental dualities: innocence and experience, good and evil, body and soul, life and death'. David Almond deals in the world we know rather than the world of fantasy, but he also acquaints us with the prime dualities: dark and light, past and present and (again), life and death, fear and its antidotes (knowledge and love).

It is unlikely that someone in the 10 to 14 age group seeking specifically for a frightening read would pick out Almond's books. The outcome in each is benign and life-affirming, with underlying values that celebrate the natural world and human relationships, family (or the memory of family, or substitute family) and friends.

Strong bonds – almost twinships – between boys and girls are another recurring element (Michael and Mina in *Skellig*, Kit and Allie in *Kit's Wilderness*, Erin and January in *Heaven Eyes*), extending traditional ideas of sisterhood and brotherhood. (In *Kit's Wilderness*, for instance, Kit Watson and John Askew, descendants of two pit children killed in a mining accident in 1821, seal a pact as blood brothers; while the children of Whitegates residential home in *Heaven Eyes* build surrogate families for each other. Erin, one of three Whitegates children who run away, forms an orphans' sisterhood with Heaven Eyes/Anna, the rootless waif whom they encounter at the end of a perilous journey.)

Throughout Almond's novels, the past (especially industrial and working-class heritage) is presented as something to be preserved and treasured. A particular value is attached to the celebration of the past in the form of an older generation's elusive memories. Death and loss (or threat of loss) are balanced by evidence of a way forward; old age is nurtured by youth. Yet each of these novels retreats at some point from the powerful human networks of Almond's fictional base to a heart of darkness into which a child protagonist travels alone. At the emotional centre of each narrative the child confronts fear of a particular intensity. The way in which fear operates in Almond's three novels is interwoven with his sense of place and history.

The outer fictional landscape in all his books for children is one of a formerly thriving industrial region of England – the north-east – which has seen its fabric and communities fall into disrepair in the post-industrial age, with decay imminent if not already set in. Children on the brink of puberty play among remnants of the past in wastelands which are poised between one useful life and, perhaps, another as yet unspecified. The clean sweep of the future will arrive before they are fully adult, and it is welcome in some ways. 'You cannot beat a bit of knocky down,' says one of the builders who demolish the garage at the end of *Skellig* (166). The setting for *Heaven Eyes* pits one bank of the Tyne which has been 'rehabilitated' into a leisure area against the opposite bank, not yet in the realm of inner-city regeneration, where the urban landscape is in the final stage of collapse. In Almond's books, children's adventures incorporate tottering walls, shivering timbers and treacherous chasms.

It is easy to imagine the appeal of settings such as the condemned garage in Michael's family's new home; the tumbledown house where he and Mina hide the strange creature, Skellig; John Askew's den in *Kit's Wilderness*, with his images of 'the gates of Heaven and the snapping jaws of hell' (6) etched on the walls; the redundant mines of Stoneygate with their perilously collapsible labyrinths; and the deadly Black Middens and crumbling quays and warehouses in *Heaven Eyes*. To the current generation of readers, an unsupervised game on an unfenced wasteland that lasts from after school until after dark is the stuff of fantasy. In each of the three novels the child players seek out the darkest, filthiest, most repulsive (to adults, that is) crannies in which to keep their play dates with terror.

Almond's inner fictional landscape must also be considered. This incorporates the inner lives of the child and adult characters including their relationship with fear, and with what Mr Chambers, the headteacher in *Kit's Wilderness*, calls 'this desire we have to be scared, to be terrified, to look into the darkness' (165): a desire which Mr Chambers himself preaches against in assembly. The ability and willingness of Almond's characters to 'look into the darkness' fluctuates with their life experience and imaginative resources. Readers are reminded at various times in these narratives of the fragility of the very old and the very young. And yet these are the points at which it could be said that the human psyche is furthest removed from terror: the baby may feel it, but does not yet have a name for it; while for the old, confusion and memory loss, in themselves genuine causes for dread, take the edge off the fear itself. The sharpest commentator on the nature of fear in these three novels is Kit's grandfather who, throughout *Kit's Wilderness*, slowly and painfully losing his mental faculties in the last months of his life, a life he has spent in the mines, where death is a whisker away. In his more lucid moments, he realizes that he is close enough to looking into the darkness to be able to describe it, which makes it hold less fear. The effects and advantages of extreme old age are in evidence in all three novels: in *Skellig*, Michael's family moves into a house previously owned by an old man, Ernie

Myers. Mr Myers is now dead and his presence is eradicated by the family's renovations, but Skellig, the secret observer hiding in the garage, remembers him. In the two later novels grandfather figures are a crucial link with the past.

Poised between the very young and the very old, children who have reached a certain level of imaginative maturity but are not yet adults are shown as prepared to explore the nature of terror. By contrast, the adults in mid-life who are the gatekeepers of children's imaginative lives, are depicted as the group least able to deal with it: they are too old to remember being children and have not yet faced their own imminent deaths. Children's fascination with the dark side of the human psyche creates genuine fears for their safety in parents and teachers, but may also be constructed as a threat to the adults' sense of control. So adults put the dens and dangerous structures out of bounds and outlaw unsavoury friends and 'weird' strangers. While, like Mr Chambers, they recommend that terror should be kept on the page and the stage, they decry the less mainstream art forms where such explorations of terror occur, including some of the publications covered elsewhere in this book (comics, horror series fiction, popular thrillers and so on).

The tension between children's legitimate fears, adults' fears for them, and adults' fears for themselves is at work throughout all three of Almond's novels for children. Each consecutive novel represents a development in where he chooses to place these factors in his fictional landscape. The treatment of fear is linked with the other major themes of children's self-development and their relationship with their roots in family and wider community. This is all a means to Almond's end, the exploration of the child's psyche and its voyage into the dark interior, a voyage which the adult reader can also share although it has particular appeal for adolescents.

The Journey of the Lost Boys: *Skellig* and *Kit's Wilderness*

Both *Skellig* and *Kit's Wilderness* open with what appears to be a fresh start: a new home, but also the threat of an imminent death in the family. In the first paragraph of *Skellig*, we encounter Dr. Death, as Michael calls the doctor who attends his ailing infant sister: 'the others were inside the house with Dr. Death, worrying about the baby' (2). The baby herself remains nameless until the final word of the novel. (How we are told characters' names and where they are placed in the narrative is important in these texts, as I discuss later in relation to the commemorative lists of the real and imagined dead children in *Kit's Wilderness* and the naming of the Whitegates children in *Heaven Eyes*.)

Dr. Death is not banished until the tale is almost over, and his presence overshadows the sense of a new beginning usually represented by moving into a new home. Michael's mother blames the house itself, inherited in a decrepit state from Mr Myers, for the baby's ills, although we later find out that the child has a weak heart.

In *Kit's Wilderness* Kit's family has also moved house in order to look after Kit's Grandpa, a retired miner whose health and mental faculties are in decline. The narrators of Almond's first two novels, Michael and Kit, are not quite adults, not quite children: they are what adults would call 'old enough to know better'. Each is trying to find a niche in a family in crisis in which it seems that they have been banished to the fringes by preoccupied, grief-stricken elders. Kit's mother tells him brusquely to 'go to school, do your duty' (64) when Grandpa is taken ill, casting Kit out into an emotional wilderness as well as a physical wilderness, the unofficial playground at the heart of their village where he encounters John Askew and his mysterious game. In *Skellig* Michael's sorrow and foreboding at his sister's illness is mingled with resentment at the attention she is absorbing and the disruption to his own priorities – investigating the presence of the mysterious Skellig and, later, curing his ills.

Michael and Kit have much in common as young adolescent boys who feel out on a limb amid families that are in general tightly knit. This may be the normal state endured by this age group, but here it is intensified by the threat of imminent loss and crisis within the family. They are both also ripe for an imaginative journey of the sort that Almond's narratives require: well-rounded boys (writers with a rich inner life and social beings, too) who are responsive to education in the broader sense.

Almond's first and second novels have in common their concern with how learning that happens in school is extended and enriched by experience in the wider world. In *Skellig* one side of a debate about the values of home-schooling versus school-based education is voiced through Michael's friend Mina, who is taught at home and despises the limits which she perceives are built into learning at school. In contrast Michael, like Kit, is a boy for whom more traditional schooling works in tandem with private exploration of ideas. He has put down firm roots at his school, which he did not change with the house move, and compares his football games at break favourably with Mina's more solitary pleasures. Kit faces the usual disadvantages of being the new boy, but swiftly overcomes them and is accepted into the élite who play the game called Death.

Formal education is seen to be crucial in supplying these boy narrators with the imaginative toolkits that equip them to survive inner upheaval and make them receptive to contemplation of life beyond the readily understood. Each encounters a key teacher who fosters his writing ability, while a school project on a mind-stretching theme supplies an extra layer of metaphor for the respective texts. In *Skellig* the added feature in Michael's mindscape is the study of evolution; in *Kit's Wilderness* Kit is inspired by the study of the ground beneath his feet from the beginning of time, which begins in geography lessons and is reinforced by his grandfather's tales of his journey to the centre of the Earth.

Writing in *The Times* about *Heaven Eyes*, Almond's third novel, Sarah Johnson notes: 'The 'inner child' is, sadly, a much-parodied concept. But David Almond believes in it passionately, and makes us believe with him.'[3] Johnson's observation applies equally to the first two novels. In the course of the path towards an encounter with the 'inner child' lies a confrontation with terror. In all three books the approach to this unknown self is through the Underworld (literally a place of overwhelming darkness, sometimes labyrinthine) which holds deep within it a chasm in which the young narrators have semi-hallucinatory experiences. Scenes such as Michael's collapse at his moment of greatest fear for his sister; Erin's moment of realization that her mother has abandoned her in spirit as well as in flesh; and Kit's vision of the dead pit children during his first experiment with John Askew's game; are staging posts on the children's lone voyages to the heart of darkness. Kit's vision, which he sees after coming round from a blackout, is one of many return visits to the mine where his ancestor died, which he makes in visions, dreams, writing and, finally, reality.

I remembered nothing, just darkness, emptiness. Pain and stiffness in my bones. Frail muscles. Crawled on all fours to the steps, reached up to draw the door aside. Then I heard the voices: little high-pitched whispers, little giggles. I stared into the darkness of the den, saw nothing but the bones, the paintings, the carvings.

I rubbed my eyes.

'Who's there?' I whispered.

The giggling intensified.

I rubbed my eyes again, squinted, and then I saw them, skinny bodies in the flickering light. They hunched in the corners at the light's edge. They blended with the walls. They shifted and faded as I tried to focus on them. But I saw their goggling eyes, their blackened skin, heard their high-pitched giggles, and I knew that they were with me, the ancient pit children, down there in the darkness of Askew's den. (*Kit's Wilderness*, 50)

Almond's employment of the fate of a frail infant in the narrative structure of *Skellig* treads a narrow line between emotional engagement and sentimentality, but it works because of the way the baby's predicament is integrated into Michael's wider imaginative universe. The boy's growing store of knowledge about the physiology of humans and birds, drawn partly from schoolwork and partly from access to Mina's wide-ranging intelligence, allows him to approach the unspeakable nucleus of his fear: namely that his sister will die.

Almond places alongside an urge to 'look into the darkness' a young adolescent's curiosity about the body and its functions. Michael studies the human skeleton in his exercise book and lets the resourceful Mina, who monitors blackbird chicks in her garden instead of doing National Curriculum tests at school, talk him through the composition of pigeons' bones, while pondering two other very different organisms. He tries to match the distorted frame of the curious creature in the back of his parents' garage, not quite human and not quite bird, to his expectation of what a human and a bird should be. He puzzles over Skellig's wings, having been told by his mother that shoulder blades are the remains of the wings which all humans once had; but when Michael finds him, Skellig is crippled with arthritis and his wings, if not clipped, are trapped beneath his filthy clothes and cramped by his living conditions. He has kept himself alive by crunching bluebottles; in better times he had scavenged Ernie Myers's leftovers. Later, with his power restored thanks to Michael and Mina's help, Skellig becomes an awe-inspiring figure, but Michael has to overcome revulsion at his animal nature: 'I caught the stench of his breath, the stench of the things the owls had given him to eat. I gagged' (110).

During the time that Michael is helping Skellig back to full strength, his sister's condition declines. Holding her in his arms before she is taken back to hospital, he is conscious of her frailty. 'I touched her skin and her tiny soft bones. I felt the place where her wings had been' (37). For much of the book Michael's sister is present in his experience as an absence, as a topic of obsessive conversation for well-meaning adults and sometimes in his imagination as one of the innocents celebrated in the poetry and paintings of William Blake (another discovery Michael has made through Mina). Studying Blake's paintings of angels at Mina's kitchen table, Michael imagines his sister as an angel-in-waiting. 'I wondered what she would see, with her innocent eyes. I wondered what she would see, if she was near to death' (123). His fears for the baby are too terrible to share with the adults who seem too preoccupied to answer them, so nobody has absolved Michael of responsibility for keeping her alive. He likens their joint predicament to that of the blackbird fledglings he has seen fighting for life in Mina's garden and identifies his body with the baby's to the extent that he is convinced that his heart is beating for them both. 'What would I feel,' he asks himself on the eve of his sister's heart operation, 'when they opened the baby's fragile chest, when they cut into her tiny heart?' (132).

Skellig has his views on babies, in fact on humans in general, which put the emphasis on life. They represent for him 'Spittle, muck, spew and tears' (28). Once in hospital Michael's sister is characterized by the absence of all of these signs of life: she is clean, quiet and subdued by technology, except in Michael's drawings which both give her life and depict the longed-for outcome of her recovery. 'I drew the baby time and again, sometimes focusing on her wide, bold, eyes, sometimes on her tiny hands, sometimes on the way her whole body arched when she rested on your knee' (11).

After listening to Mina's mother tell the story of Persephone, Michael braces his strength for his own journey through the Underworld by reflecting on the goddess's own perseverance through a state of terror. 'She squeezed through black tunnels. She took wrong turnings, banged her head against the rocks. Sometimes she gave up in despair and she just lay weeping in the pitch darkness. But she struggled on' (138). Feeling at his weakest, Michael goes with Mina to the empty house where they have installed the recovering Skellig to ask him for help, but he has vanished. Michael first faints from sheer terror, then comes round and senses that his heart has stopped beating for the baby.

Terror is a strong force in this story but one kept on a tight rein by Skellig in his guardian angel role and by the intensely alive, outward-looking Mina. It later becomes clear that when Skellig went missing he was watching over the sick infant. Mina takes a similar view to Skellig on the basic needs of humans: 'We're still like chicks,' she said. 'Happy half the time, half the time dead scared' (132).

Skellig is neither child nor adult (before he is cured he has an ancient physique and a child's needs). With his super-adult powers, he seems a safe repository for Michael's fears and can help to resolve them where adults cannot. A parent's ultimate fear is the loss of a child, and Michael's venture into what his parents would perceive as a dangerous area of the psyche would induce as much anxiety as the baby's weak heart. The child's voyage into the Underworld is just as frightening, perhaps more, for the adults who wait on the surface, and the adults cannot call on Skellig for help.

In Almond's second novel, terror is allowed off the leash and this time it's of Rottweiler proportions. While *Skellig*, which introduced the myth of Persephone, opens 'just in time for the spring' (2), *Kit's Wilderness* charts the winter months of Persephone's absence, starting with 'the day the clocks went back' and reaching its emotional heart around the winter equinox. The setting is Stoneygate, a village built on fear; literally on top of a disused mine, which shows itself as cracks in the walls and roads and shards of coal in the soil, and provides an uneasy bedrock for the local children's games. For generations of miners and their families, fear is part of the dangerous job and looking it in the face with equanimity is an acquired skill. The grandfather of the narrator, Kit Watson, belongs to the last generation able to spend a life working in the mine. He tells Kit:

> As a lad I'd wake up trembling, knowing that as a Watson born in Stoneygate I'd soon be following my ancestors into the pit ... There was more to it than just the fear, Kit. We were also driven to it. We understood our fate. There was the strangest joy in dropping down together into the darkness that we feared. And most of all there was the joy of coming out again together into the lovely world. (19)

The account of Persephone's journey that sustained Michael in *Skellig* pre-empts the in-depth study in *Kit's Wilderness* of the physical nature of the Underworld, of the land below Stoneygate and the resilience of its people.

> She fought through bedrock and clay and iron ore and coal, through fossils of ancient creatures, the skeletons of dinosaurs, the buried remains of ancient cities. She burrowed past the tangled roots of great trees. She was torn and bleeding but she kept telling herself to move onward and upward. She told herself that soon she'd see the light of the sun again and feel the warmth of the world again. (*Skellig*, 138)

The mining disaster of 1821 is a collective tragedy in the Stoneygate history. The Watsons and the Askews are among the old families whose children were sent to work in the mine, and killed in the accident. Kit is returning to his roots when his family moves back to Stoneygate. He is picked out both as a kindred spirit and as a member of an ancient family by John Askew, the wild boy of the village whose family is traditionally shunned, currently because his father, barred from the experiences and occupation provided by the mine, has turned to drink and violence. 'He's just one of them that has been wasted', as Grandpa tells Kit (110). Young Askew also presides over 'the game called Death', clad, appropriately, in a T-shirt bearing the word 'Megadeth'. Today's Stoneygate children are not sent down the mine, and this game is what they do instead.

The game called Death has much to fascinate children and alarm adults. Being asked to participate is considered a badge of honour. Only children from the old families are eligible. Kit qualifies, but is still only allowed to undergo the initiation ceremony under John's protection. The names of the elect – those who have 'died' in the game – are etched on the wall of John's den in a homage to the roster of the dead of 1821 in the churchyard.

Death is a traditional punchline in children's games (from Ring o'Roses to Murder in the Dark) and this one has everything: suspense as the circle of children wait for the spinning bottle to select the day's 'dead one' and Kit murmurs to himself *'me, not me, me, not me'* (48) and drama in John's ritual, in which he casts himself as master of ceremonies and high priest and solicits pre-determined responses from the 'dead one'. ' "There will be a death this day ... " "Do you abandon life?" "I abandon life" "Do you truly wish to die?" "I truly wish to die" ... "All you see and all you know will disappear. It is the end. You will be no more" ' (49).

The game follows the pattern of a dare game with a hoax element. The 'dead one' is left alone in the pitch-dark den for as long as it takes him to realize he is not dead, while the others wait outside, at the gates of the Underworld, for him to emerge. The 'death' itself, which can last for minutes or hours, is in the 'dead' player's imagination. Through heightened ritual and sheer force of personality, John creates a climate in which even those who suspect a hoax will be too frightened to expose it, or unwilling to give up the kudos attached to participation. 'It was like nothing. It was like being nothing' (56), Kit tells his friend Allie (untruthfully, as it turns out) after his first 'death' in the den. For most participants there is, literally, nothing to be frightened of, but the nothing itself is the truly frightening factor. The fear is intensified by the power dynamic between the leader, the players as a group and the players as individuals. For John, the game is a way to assert the authority that he cannot acquire through a more respectable route because of his family's reputation.

The game pits the individual – the 'dead one' – against the living group, in a balance of power familiar to the bullied child. One way for a quick-witted 'dead one' to gain an advantage is to demonstrate more nerve than the living: to delay the resurrection until the players waiting in the open air become more scared than the player left below. Allie, the would-be actress, boasts of having double-bluffed the living, even John the ringleader, by emerging long after her expected time limit with an invented account of after-death experiences which eclipse anything in John's vivid imagination.

Grandpa recognizes in Allie 'one that's filled with light and life' (62). Her strong sense of self preserves her from psychological control by John and she seems immune to the weight of the past while Kit and John are drawn to it. Allie is more concerned with her immediate future, and in planning her escape from Stoneygate. Her fears centre around not managing to escape, not being as great as she believes she can be, having her wings clipped by sarcastic teachers. Although she wants to be an actress and is able to transform herself at will, her creativity is more self-absorbed and of the moment than Kit's or John's, whose words and pictures are fuelled by their common history. Allie is from an old family too, but she feels sufficiently free from her history to tamper with the rules of the game called Death for dramatic effect.

When Kit's turn comes to 'die' he does not have to invent a tale to carry back to the living, but he does not want to share his experience. While in the den he has a vision of the ancient pit children who died in 1821, which he withholds from his report to Allie. When he tries to return to this unexplored territory in a later round of the game, he is hauled out in mid-death by a concerned teacher and, under the rules, sentenced to 'a living death' (77), with the questions he wanted to ask his predecessors left unanswered. In another grim roll call, the teacher declaims the names of the players fleeing from the den, whose peril is now one of the living world, namely that they are in big trouble at school. John is expelled after the resulting investigation and disappears, in hiding from his father. This round of the game is over, but John and Kit must play on.

The adults' reaction to the children's exploration of the psychic underworld is to push the darkness back by blocking up the den and getting rid of the ringleader. They encourage the right sort of imaginative play: Kit's stories are acceptable but John's exceptional artwork is not, for the moment, acceptable enough to save his school career.

The dead of 1821 (including Silky, the mischievous pit child of local legend who surfaces in Kit's writing, inspired by his grandfather's tales of life in the mine) continue to haunt Kit through the winter as Grandpa's faculties diminish along with the hours of daylight. In particular, Kit is aware of the children whose bodies could not be rescued for burial and whose 'waking death' is similar to Kit's own state of inner confusion. John has seen them too, and returns briefly from hiding (by which point he is widely believed to be really dead) to tell Kit: 'The earth can't hold its dead. They rise and watch us. They draw us to them ... This is why you're like me ... Because we know about the darkness of the past, because we know about the darkness of the dead' (170).

Early in the novel, when Kit's grandfather is still able to take the boy on a tour of his heritage, he recalls his generation's version of the game called Death. He is the adult who knows most about Kit's activities in the den, and the only one who does not disapprove. Rather, he is playful and conspiratorial as he reveals how in his day the village children would enact their own subversive and sacrilegious ritual at the graveyard memorial to the dead of 1821.

> 'Used to get a laugh here long ago,' he said. 'Used to come at night as kids. Used to dance in a ring round the monument and chant the Our Father backwards. Used to say we'd see the faces of those old pit kids blooming in the dark.' He giggled. 'Bloody terrifying. Used to belt home laughing and screaming, scared half to death. Kids' games, eh? What they like?' (21)

He compares his periods of memory loss, of absenteeism from the world, to 'following Silky': the elusive golden-haired child of the mine being a metaphor for the false glimmer of memory that leads the old man into the darkest part of the labyrinth, then abandons him. 'The more you stand there the more the darkness comes into you, till there's nothing but the darkness, and you don't see nothing, you don't hear nothing, you don't remember nothing.' Kit, recognising his own 'death' experience in Grandpa's account, prompts him: 'And you're not scared till you come back,' and he replies, 'Scared to find out that you've been away at all. Scared to think you'll be going away again. But when you're there ... nothing' (62).

Later in the novel, after Grandpa's first major collapse, Kit himself follows Silky in a dreamlike vision. Led to the heart of the mine, he finds Grandpa near death, but revives him. Together they relive the darkest hour of Stoneygate's dead children who by now are visiting Kit regularly, but there is a happier outcome in the vision, for rescue is on the way: 'I held him tight for hours, for a million years, till at last we heard the footsteps in the tunnel, saw the distant light of the lamps, heard the voices of the men who'd come to find us' (96). This vision offers Kit the key to tackling his fear of the horrors of the past. If he can summon the strength to enter the labyrinth, the community on the surface will be strong enough to save him.

Present-day Stoneygate has its own child who is lost, feared dead: as

Christmas approaches, John Askew does not come home and his mother, clutching another fragile baby to her breast, grieves in his absence while recognising in Kit the ability to find him. More lost children appear in two parallel tales that slice through temporal and geological layers. The first is the short story that Kit works on through the winter, set in ancient times in the area now called Stoneygate. Like Michael in *Skellig*, Kit is a writer, and he makes sense of his experiences and challenges his fear through his writing. In the story a family travelling south to escape perpetual winter finds shelter in a cave, similar to John's underground hiding place in the disused mine, which Kit visits later. The son of the family, a boy called Lak who, like John, is at loggerheads with his father, rescues his baby sister from a bear which he kills with his dead grandfather's axe. He then carries his sister south on the trail of the fleeing family, who have given the pair up for dead.

Meanwhile Allie stars in the school play, a retelling of Andersen's fairy tale *The Snow Queen*. The setting is a frozen wilderness in which the Snow Queen's splinter of ice transforms a loving sister into an ice girl who turns against her brother (the sibling roles of Andersen's original tale are reversed). While Allie works her stage magic above ground, lost in an inner wilderness for the sake of the chilly midwinter tale, John is marooned below ground in a dangerous drift mine nursing his hatred, which has the immobilizing effect of the wicked queen's ice fragment. When he summons Kit to meet him there, it's a cry for help couched as a challenge.

John both resents and needs Kit, who can lead him towards reconciliation with his family; Kit both fears and needs John and his commitment to their shared history. The sense of having been entrusted with a mission, by both Mrs Askew in real life and Lak's mother in the dreams that inspire his story, provides the spur that Kit needs to venture into the recesses of the mine where the pit children died, the territory he first marked out when he played the game in John's den. His meeting with John is both a final confrontation with terror and a sealing of their blood brotherhood.

Midwinter night is followed by dawn. The two temporarily lost children, Kit and John, emerge from the pit like the miners of recent history for whom the end of each shift was a signal that they had survived another day of living death. The boys' return to the surface represents a turning point. Grandpa, who is near to death but still listening for the rescue party that just might reach him in the labyrinth, finally accepts that this time the men with the lamps will not arrive. Before the clocks go forward again in Stoneygate, he has died. John is making a fresh start with his father, who has stopped drinking, and with school. Kit and John, like Kit's creation, Lak, have all triumphed over terror and moved on enriched by it, sustained by the life above ground. The mine has been made safe and its history will not die with Grandpa's generation. The school parties that visit still shriek when the lights go out, but the pit children are at peace.

The Journey of the Damaged Children: *Heaven Eyes*

Heaven Eyes extends the theme of balance between the fear that the wilderness of the mind holds for the old and the energy of youth which, for the worn-out spirit, represents the searchlights of the rescue party. The senile man whom the foundling, Heaven Eyes, knows as Grampa, has passed beyond the stage of confusion suffered by Kit's grandfather. Grampa is fond of saying that 'Tomorrow will shed light', but for him this is not to be. He also frequently says that he is 'all befuddled again'. Once caretaker of a printing works beside the Tyne, Grampa continues to squat at the derelict premises, which have retained their epic grandeur. He is alone until he rescues from the Black Middens mudflats a small child whom he names Heaven Eyes ''cos she does see through all the trouble in the world to the Heaven that does lie beneath' (69).

He feeds her on the contents of abandoned packing cases, teaches her his haunting and earthy speech patterns and increasingly relies on her for his frail hold on understanding. She learns to perceive people of the wider world as 'ghosts' and to forget her real name and the family whose boat sank on the Tyne. The first humans besides Grampa that she meets in her new existence are three children called Erin Law, January Carr and Mouse Gullane, who have run away from Whitegates children's home. Erin, the narrator, introduces the Whitegates group: 'We are damaged children, but we are happy' (70).

Their parents have died or abandoned them, depriving them of what is understood to be a happy childhood. Erin's mother has died, her father was a one-night stand; Mouse has been tattooed with the words 'Please look after me', in a cruel parody of Paddington Bear's label; January is named after 'the bitter month in which he was found' on the steps of a hospital (4). Names are important to these children: their names are all they have. Indeed, Erin asserts her own by opening the story 'My name is Erin Law' (3) in a homage to the first line of Herman Melville's *Moby Dick*. Later, Mouse lovingly spells out their names with stray characters from the redundant type trays in what is now Grampa's printing works.

The efforts of social services have proved unequal to the children's needs. Maureen, the inadequate housemother at Whitegates, expects

Erin to look after her. Her textbook strategies of Circle Time and Life Story books cannot contain the extremes of her charges' experiences although she tells them, disingenuously, 'We want you to be frightened of nothing' (13). Erin and January make the most of their few advantages over less 'damaged' children: they have learned to look out for each other and they are not well supervised, and therefore able to run away from Whitegates for adventures that might last an afternoon or a few nights. They relish the game that they play with the authorities, compete good-naturedly with the other children ('Nobody had tried going off on a raft before', (11)), and plan each time to stay away forever but, when they are caught, calmly wait for the next chance to escape. Their lust for freedom is not unlike that expressed by Allie in *Kit's Wilderness*, but their 'damaged' status frees them to act on it. They are not afraid of being lost, alone or forgotten, because they are all these things already. There is nothing to stop them from embarking on an expedition that might be envied by better protected child readers. Joined by Mouse, they sail down the Tyne on a raft that January has made from salvaged doors appropriately labelled 'Entrance', 'Danger' and 'Exit' and carrying his graphic warning, 'MAy anyWOn whO StEEls thiS rAFT be FerrYD StRAte to HELL!' (33).

The Black Middens where the raft delivers them are hellish indeed. They are treacherous mudflats in the shallows of the Tyne, alongside Grampa's decaying dockside kingdom. The stretch of collapsing printing works and warehouses awaiting development is opposite a developed area where 'a bit of knocky-down' has cleared space for the trappings of civilized life including restaurants, pubs and cycle tracks; within earshot of the raft, but a world away to the Whitegates children as the game turns against them and they nearly perish in the mud. When Heaven Eyes rescues them and persuades Grampa, a grotesque figure wielding a giant shovel, not to dig them back into the slime, they pass from the dubious state of being 'in care' to the realm of the caretaker.

The label on Grampa's jacket reads 'SECURITY' and that is what he represents for *Heaven Eyes* and for Mouse, whom he swiftly adopts as his 'Little Helper'. He is still carrying out his official duties of patrolling the quayside and seeing off intruders or 'ghosts', but he also trawls the Middens for treasure, logging his finds in his ancient ledger. His evocative entry for the arrival of the Whitegates children, made on a Friday, although he says 'call it Tuesday', reads:

Discoveries, several. Three plates, broken. One cup, broken. One pan, no handle. Two coins amounting to two new pence and one old penny. A bag of bread, sodden. Umpteen pop bottles, plastic. One boot, one sock, one pair Y-fronts, extra large. One wing, kittiwake. One dog, black, dead. One large thigh bone, source unknown. Jewellery, none. Riches, none. Mysteries, one. (67)

Grampa's authoritative book with its official-looking ruled columns is his substitute for memory and a record of the life that continues in a place that has been declared no longer useful by the outside world, and of the lost and displaced objects no longer remembered by the 'ghosts' who once owned them. 'Names. They have names, so fast forgotten,' he says (60) committing Erin, January and Mouse to posterity by logging them in the pages that also contain Heaven Eyes's Life Story, semi-literate but more truthful than the contents of the Whitegates files. The 'dark and wet and filthy tale' of Heaven Eyes's 'birth' out of the Black Middens is not easy to access. In less 'befuddled' times, Grampa filed the dossier he had compiled on her out of her reach. Erin, Mouse and January, who become her substitute family, appear to her to have been 'born' from the mud in the same way. For Heaven Eyes, 'Only the twilight zone symbolised by the shifting, muddy foreshore, exists.'[4] The riverside cyclists she can see having a jolly day out on the opposite bank belong to a 'ghost' world which she has learned is not for her. As she gets closer to Erin, she reveals that 'in my sleep thoughts I is like a ghost ... I is with them that is like ghosts' (128) and discloses her real name, Anna, 'my fibbing and imagining name' (129).

Heaven Eyes is the victim of benign neglect and, in developmental terms, more 'damaged' than Erin, January or Mouse. She has spent perhaps as long as ten years with Grampa, hidden from potential rescuers. When Kit's grandfather sensed that his mind was in retreat, he urged Kit: 'keep me with you' (62). Grampa repeatedly makes it clear that he is prepared to 'fettle' (kill) the child visitors to keep Heaven Eyes. Her consciousness is that of a child too young to feel fear (which makes Grampa all the more anxious to bask in her light in the hope that she will keep befuddlement at bay), but she does suffer agonies over the separation from her family. This is a pain that the Whitegates children can share, but they are sustained by their more recent memories as well as by each other while Heaven Eyes has been struggling alone. Thanks to her bond with Erin, and the salvaged family photograph that January finds in Grampa's stores, she has begun to retrieve her past from her 'sleep thoughts', but the interval that she spent close to death in the Black Middens is the long-buried and unspeakable terror that will only surface 'slow as slow' (193). Heaven Eyes's journey towards the chapter of her Life Story that Grampa has not been able to document has just begun when the novel ends.

Grampa has kept his record because he knows Heaven Eyes will eventually have to leave him. He dies having overcome his dread of the inevitable, and she leaves with the Whitegates children just as the demolition crews invade Grampa's kingdom. Erin, too, has completed a chapter of the 'dark and wet and filthy tale' that is her own Life Story. The various terrors of the Black Middens (including the body of a dead quayside worker, petrified in the mud), Grampa's instability and the knife that he keeps in his drawer seem paltry when measured against the emotional baggage Erin has brought with her on January's raft, namely the conviction that her mother's memory will one day no longer sustain her. She chooses the most remote corner of the forsaken industrial empire for her own voyage into darkness. Her load is lighter on the return journey to Whitegates: she, too, has absorbed some of Heaven Eyes's light and will soon start to need her mother less. But first, she must contemplate the terrifying extent of her loss.

> I imagined beasts staring out at me from the deepest darkest places ... They were creatures that had grown in darkness and desolation, mutant life forms, half-dead and half-alive. They grabbed at me as I passed by, they hissed my name, they tried to drag me to them, tried to make me theirs ... I went down, down. Ancient crumbling steps. The stench of damp and rot and doom. I went down into the deepest darkness until there was nowhere left to go, just the furthest corner of the furthest cellar. I lay down in the slime.
> 'Mum,' I whispered.
> No answer. (98)

'It's only a game' (*Facetaker*, 59): *Transformer* and *Facetaker* by Philip Gross

The fictional territory just visited in David Almond's novels presents the reader with powerful young people who confront and defeat their inner anxieties supported by friends of different but equal strength and sustained by their own imaginative resources, by enlightenment drawn from previous generations or by the collective strength and goodwill of their communities. They seek out external sources of the desired frisson of fear by daring to investigate strange noises in the out-of-bounds garage, playing the game called Death and launching a flimsy raft on the hazardous Tyne, but the underlying fear is the internal and ancient dread of death and loss, dramatized in John Askew's game. The individuals who at some point pose immediate threats to the protagonists, notably John Askew in *Kit's Wilderness* and Grampa in *Heaven Eyes*, are not predators and are only threatening in one aspect of their personality.

Philip Gross's novels *Transformer* (1996) and *Facetaker* (1999) feature loosely knit groups of contemporary adolescents who, in common with Almond's characters, seek out diversions, rituals and strategies for escape. The fears and dangers that they are then exposed to are more concrete than those outlined earlier in this chapter but no less complex. The evils that beset them are those of parents' nightmares: self-abuse; manipulation by plausible villains; encounters with unsavoury characters on the streets after curfew. At the outset, the protagonists themselves dread boredom above everything else, and Gross's acknowledgment of this is a key factor in the books' appeal to young readers who will also enjoy their gripping plots, strong narrative voices and acute depiction of uneasy alliances on the margins of the safe adult world.

Transformer is the name of an amateur rock band with dreams of the big break, which finds itself at the centre of a tale of self-destruction and distorted egotism. Emod, the teenage boy who starts the band with his friend Ben, recalls the band's encounter with Hugo, a charlatan with New Age trappings who becomes *Transformer's* manager. Similarly, the central figure who drives the action of *Facetaker* embodies both charisma and cruelty. Denzil is a young man with exceptional talent for orchestrating mayhem, who recruits Jon, the narrator, Jon's cousin Sarah and Sarah's friend Claire to assist in a macabre experiment involving the photo booth at their town's railway station.

In *Transformer* the threat to the group's well-being comes from an adult outsider, while in *Facetaker* the less culpable but no less destructive villain is not only one of the group but responsible for forming it. In each novel, Gross pays close attention to the preoccupations of the group and the dynamics within it, and to the vulnerability of certain members. These titles are in the Point Horror Unleashed series, comprised of works that are longer and more sophisticated than most Point Horror titles. Gross has written an excellent dystopian fantasy novel, *Psylicon Beach*, but the predicaments faced in the texts considered here are firmly connected to life in the present with only a brief suspension of disbelief required for some aspects of their resolution (such as the discovery at the end of *Facetaker* that Denzil, the compulsive liar, may have been telling the truth about his shaky premise for the photo booth game). The psychological depth of these novels, and the multiple layers of meaning of *Transformer* in particular, will increase their appeal to readers in their mid-teens.

The consistent sense of place and heritage as an active force in David Almond's novels is not present in these novels: the initial settings are intended to be Anytowns, dull on the surface with a seedy substrata that is itself stereotypical, but within which extraordinary things can happen. The terror of the environment for these young people with their dread of ennui, lies in its ordinariness. Gross uses changes in perspective to heighten drama by showing the apparently ordinary anew. For instance, in *Transformer* Hugo shows Ben and Emod their home town from above, hovering beside them like Satan, in order to bend them to his will. Later, the band goes on the road to Cornwall and Gross uses the new location as a device to increase the group's sense of entrapment.

Gross's characters are a crucial couple of years older than Almond's and so are at the stage of deliberately testing their boundaries. They have more in common with Allie, who wants to escape from a life sentence in Stoneygate, than with Kit, Michael or Erin. Typically Gross's protagonists have no sense of coming from anywhere: their history is to be escaped from rather than discovered. Denzil, the arch-manipulator in *Facetaker*, has a 'backstory' rather than a history, which can only be guessed at.

The fears that are common in adolescents but that most adults have left behind or suppressed are at the heart of these novels: on the one hand fear of not being accepted, not fitting in; on the other of failing to stand out from the herd, of being an also-ran, of vanishing among the masses into averageness and blandness. Part of the mixture of emotions is the paradoxical fear of not being understood on one hand, yet on the other, of being understood too well, either by parents or by an adversary who discerns and exploits one's worst fears (as Hugo does during his first encounter with Emod and Ben).

Although most of Gross's players live in conventional families (and Jon in *Facetaker* retreats to his when his adventures get out of hand), their families are not nurturing in the sense of feeding a sense of heritage or identity that will sustain them through crisis. They have average parents whose responses are average, clichéd and inappropriate. Jon's parents assume that he is on drugs; his father tries to make a shabby bargain with him to cover up his own dubious activities. Alia, the new singer in the band Transformer, is studying obsessively and starving herself, but her parents fail to act.

When *Transformer* opens in an Anytown called Borsley, near Luton, Ben asserts his individuality by insisting on sixth-form college rather than school and getting a strange haircut. Emod has constructed his own identity as the indispensable and good-hearted 'man with the van' (the roadie, below the drummer in the band's pecking order, but a wizard at electronics). Hugo in *Transformer* and Denzil in *Facetaker* each acquire a group of followers who are desperate for a reprieve from the unremarkable and ripe for the intervention of a gamemaster recruiting acolytes to participate in a very exclusive game in which the unremarkable is banished along with the average, the bland and the everyday. The more demanding the gamemaster and the more stringent the rules, the greater the attraction of the charmed circle for the recruits, who are used to observing their own strict criteria for social acceptability. In both books the narrator is a young man who sees himself as ordinary and resents it. Emod in *Transformer* and Jon in *Facetaker* are initially no better equipped than their friends against the lure of the gamemaster, although they retain a degree of scepticism (Emod more consistently than Jon). Later, however, they are responsible for puzzling out the real rules and piecing together the facts that expose the gamemaster as a fake with his own agenda and establish the threat that he represents.

As well as the name of a band, 'transformer' is a term meaning a conduit for power, and a crucial theme in the novel is power in the senses of both influence and energy. It swiftly emerges that 15-year-old Alia is under the influence of Hugo, a considerably older man, that her ground-breaking songs and impressive stage persona have been inspired by working with him in his meditation group for 'enquiring spirits' (65), which he advertises with the slogan 'Transform Your Life', and that she is his route to the control of the band. Hugo is bitter about the collapse of his own career and wants revenge on the man he holds responsible, who is now running a rock festival in Cornwall. He exploits the band members' longing for the bright lights, or at least a Saturday night slot at a festival far from Borsley, in order to make use of them in his game plan.

Transformer presents Alia as at risk both from anorexia and Hugo (who, with his stern features, motorbike and black leather cape, appears at various points as a vampire or angel of death figure). She meets him via Borsley's only gateway to alternative culture, the Arcana café, patronised by 'Beansprouts' whom Emod and Ben reject as uncool, although they are guilty of no more than drinking herbal tea, being vague and selling tarot cards. She sees the Transform Your Life flyer in the café at around the same time that she joins the band – at a point when she is is both particularly vulnerable, having just changed schools because of bullying at her last one, and desperate to reinvent

herself. Alia used to be called Natalia, but she loses some of her name
in the way that she later sacrifices a hank of her hair to what Hugo
teaches her to call 'the power': a mixture of the effects of her own
focused intelligence and the uplifting feelings that she has experienced
in Hugo's classes while listening to his homilies on shamanism.

Gradually, Gross reveals that the heightened sensations that she
attributes to 'the power' are the hallucinatory side effects of starvation.
Her shrinking body is part of the sacrifice: an academic high achiever
with social insecurity and a terror of again carrying the despised bulk
that exists only in her imagination, Alia is a prime candidate for
anorexia, and fasting is the only route to a new self that she sees open
to her. Her perverse relish at her body's deterioration is well situated in
the horror genre. After fasting for more than a month, she shines a
torch through her hand to examine her diminished flesh: 'Her eyes
glowed with excitement, not horror, at the shadows of her own bones
and the thin layer of flesh that glowed orangey-red as if it was on fire'
(150).

She could have gained confidence slowly but safely through
performing with the band but she chooses to let Hugo fast-track her
metamorphosis. Her intensity and capacity for concentration (which
could be channeled to more positive ends) make her an apt pupil who
shares with her teacher an unfortunate passion for control. Alia
associates control of her body through starvation with elevation to the
more powerful, more spiritual state that Hugo indicates is within her
reach. It is a cruel irony that as an anorexia sufferer she is nothing
special, but one of a misguided multitude. 'You don't get it, do you?'
she says when Emod visits her in hospital. 'I nearly made it. I was
nearly perfect. Nearly special. Nearly . . . *wonderful*. If I can't be that . . .
why be anything?' (185).

Hugo promises to teach Alia to 'fly', in the sense of transcending her
body (as she already does on stage) and, by implication, for real. Flying
is a metaphor for omnipotence which is also at work in Melvin
Burgess's *Junk*, another novel published in 1996 in which Gemma, one
of a group of young drug addicts, becomes addicted to heroin because
she wants to 'fly', and Hugo's involvement with the band makes them
focused enough to 'fly' in performance. His abuse of Alia and, to a
lesser extent, Ben and Emod is psychological: he undermines their
sense of self in order to rally them to his cause and ensure that they will
not want their old lives back. The gamemaster's game plan is to win
over sceptics by targeting the cracks in their self-esteem. Thus he lures
Ben and Emod to his lair on the roof of the shopping mall, uncannily
threatening them with their own worst fears.

'If you don't come?' he said to Ben. 'Then you will be an ordinary young man, in an ordinary rock band. Only, unlike most of them, you will know to the end of your days how hopelessly ordinary you are. And how you threw away your chance … to fly. And you?' He meant me. 'You'll tinker with your electrical gadgets until the day you die. An oddball. The sad old geezer parents tell their children not to talk to.' (58)

Hugo claims to be a caretaker, and if he is he interprets his brief freely. Strangely, there are uniformed security guards in the daytime but the night watch is entrusted to Hugo, who is allowed to operate from a fire-hazard-ridden shack on the roof instead of being allocated a tidy Portakabin. Emod's first Transform Your Life class is his last, but it reveals to the reader, if not to Emod, that the sceptical man with the van may have greater psychic powers than Hugo or Alia, and that Hugo has misread him. In a vision, Emod foresees both the scene of destruction that Hugo plans to orchestrate at his enemy's festival, and the circumstances of the gamemaster's eventual death.

There was a thin mingled hissing, almost too high for the ear to hear, that started like the starlings but turned into human voices wailing, far below. Then there were lower whoops and wails: fire engines and ambulances, red lights and blue lights flashing … Then the scream was all around me, not human any more. The grey bird opened its billhook beak as it smelt burnt flesh, it shrieked like the voice of its victims and I staggered as it swooped towards me, its wing brushed my face and it wheeled out in the smoke that rose around us through the night. I was grabbing at handholds, missing, and the bird's shriek was my own cry as I teetered on the edge, then fell. (70)

Emod's reaction is much like Kit's when he emerged from John Askew's den after his 'death'. ' "Nothing," I said. I heard the screams. I smelt the burning. No, don't think … I took a deep breath. "Nothing *happened*," I said' (71). A chink forms in his resistance to 'the power', he subsequently gives the young reader a trustworthy account of Hugo's influence at work. Ben is dazzled by the older man's confidence and the names he drops. Geek, the stroppy drummer, who is unimpressed by Ben's new mentor, is replaced by a drum machine. Clive, the bass player who relates to his amp better than to humans, has the highest resistance to both Alia and Hugo but is won over in Cornwall when Hugo presents himself as a poor jobbing musician at the mercy of the record companies' money men. Hugo's influence is strongest in Cornwall. He installs the band in a cramped cottage which once belonged to a hermit called Horan, who had some healing powers but died when his neighbours forced him to attempt to fly from a rock ledge above a waterfall, now called Horan's Leap. Emod considers where putting their trust in Hugo has led them.

> I looked back into the darkness of the coffin-door. Somewhere far in the past we'd wanted something, or Ben had, at least. Yes, to get out of Borsley, that was it. Something to do with freedom. And every step we'd gone had taken us somewhere smaller – the Arcana café, the shack on the mall roof, all of us crammed in the back of the van, and now this. You bet I wanted air. (111)

Hugo may have studied shamanism and he has some of the right props, such as the ritual drum and the rare recording of 'A throat-singer of the Kekyut tribe of Western Siberia' (64). He uses a fine set of pseudo-epigrams, including 'It's only fear that keeps you in your cage' (56), 'Real power is nothing to do with right and wrong' (66), and 'Disgust is Mother Nature's last desperate effort to control us' (133), but he has none of the humility of a genuine spiritual leader. His contempt for the 'dull commonplace soul' he perceives Emod to be (189) is that of a former celebrity terrified of his own commonplace nature. At the ancient pagan site behind Horan's cottage, which is real where so much else in Hugo's world is bogus, he is shown to be no match for Horan's descendant, Mary Field, who is steeped in the lore that he dabbles in. 'Go on,' she tells him, 'show your little disciples what you really are. Their great guru ... a bully, a fraud' (134). Her challenge follows a ritual in which he has delivered the abuser's classic line, 'All real power is secret. And if anyone betrayed it, we would have to punish him' (131), and it forces him to acknowledge his limits: when Alia is drawn to Horan's Leap, he prevents her from trying to fly. By this point, Emod has discovered that another young woman in Hugo's past has died in a similar experiment and that his feud with the festival promoter stems from this episode.

This carefully drawn portrait is highly unflattering, but it does not downplay Hugo's glamour or the intrepid role model he presents to young people who are still trying on their identities and who are dazzled by the new horizons he presents to them. For adults, the terror at the heart of *Transformer* is the knowledge that they cannot protect their children against exploitation once the children are old enough to choose their own associates. For the young reader, it is the crumbling of an idol and the sense of betrayal it brings.

These anxieties are embedded in a plot outwardly centred around

the division of loyalties within the band and the startling manifestations of Alia's power: when she is challenged or under pressure she
delivers a high-pitched scream that blows electric circuits, fells
opponents and, in the one instance that does not have a rational
explanation, repairs a disabled engine. She starts small, short-circuiting
Ben's street during a rehearsal in his parents' garage, and works up to
causing havoc with Glastonbury-scale PA systems. Emod, with his
confiding, bloke-ish tone, weighs the evidence for electrical faults on
one hand and sinister forces at work on the other. Of the first disrupted
rehearsal, he says:

> I'm not one of your mystic-artistic types, no way. I believe in
> explanations, but the only explanation that made sense, at the
> moment, was that *she had made it happen*. Somehow that was
> when I began to be worried about Alia for real. (39)

Later, pondering the cause of the larger-scale disaster which was
instigated by Hugo to wreck the festival and which resulted in mass
panic and injuries, possibly deaths, Emod asks: 'If it was lightning, like
they said afterwards, why wasn't there thunder? Or maybe it was
drowned by the screech of all the amps before they blew?' (164)

Through Emod's sensible, soothing evaluation, Gross swings the
balance of probability in favour of coincidence and electrical fault, then
allows Emod unwittingly to offer a fresh reading of Transformer's
history. He is the only band member to have glimpsed the white owl
which he assumes is Alia's familiar, but which the reader could
interpret as a benign force shadowing Emod himself through times of
crisis. *Transformer* works at a third, and rewarding, narrative level
when it charts the progress of the intelligent and under-rated 'man
with the van' as he breaks free from a life as Ben's sidekick in which he
could not even use his real name (Benedict, we discover in the closing
pages) because Ben got there first. The band was Emod's idea, and
Emod has kept it on the road electronically and emotionally, soothing
wounded egos and fiddling with wires, yet it is perceived as Ben's band.
As Alia begins to recover she is also addressing readers who may be
drawn towards self-transformation when she tells Emod: 'You've got a
right to be who you are' (192).

Facetaker, Philip Gross's more recent novel (1998), opens in a
railway station: a territory of transition, full of potential for adventure,
but also for danger, the first place to go if you want to escape. However,
the tragic dénouement is the only action that involves catching a train:
the characters live their lives while waiting to leave. For Denzil's
acolytes the station is the point of departure for a journey into the

world of transients and drifters which co-exists alongside the narrator Jon's world of irritating siblings, a Mr Nice reputation at school ('How many times had I heard it? *Jon? Oh, he's OK, he's nice, you'll like him.* Why did it make me want to scream?' (47)) and a part-time job at the supermarket checkout. He despises all of it and admires his classmate Denzil, the essence of cool who makes things happen.

The photo booth (Jon calls it the Facetaker, despite Denzil's mockery) is a magnet for those who seek transformation, risk and adventure but cannot travel too far. As Gross's Prologue states: '*No one likes the pictures that it shows them but they come – somehow they have to – all the same*' (2). When Denzil and Jon find the dead body of Alice, a bedraggled homeless woman, inside the booth on their way home from school, Denzil also discovers the machine's last set of prints: pictures of a young and beautiful female. He persuades his hangers-on, Jon, Sarah and Claire, to accept his theory that these are images of Alice's *doppelgänger* and that the Facetaker will yield more pictures of the subjects' alternative identities (their true, more attractive selves, is the promise) in return for a sacrifice. Denzil suggests a drop of blood but, greedy for the potential to transform themselves, the participants deliver increasingly challenging offerings: personal treasures, creatures that have to be killed in front of the camera.

Like *Transformer*, *Facetaker* has a plot based on assumption and plausibility, driven by the desire of youth to be transformed and to try on other identities. The photo booth pictures can be customised by Sarah, Jon's talented and deceptively mild-mannered cousin, to offer the subject a choice of distorted faces to adopt. A deluded beggar whom Denzil names VI (for Village Idiot) leads the group to a store of jumble-sale-reject clothes which they use in elaborate dressing-up and acting-out games. Denzil plants the idea ('Don't you get that feeling . . . that you'd like to try, just try, being somebody else?' (73)), and his followers pick it up and run with it. They prowl the streets after curfew to try out their more dangerous selves and meet other dangerous people. Claire becomes a shoplifter, Sarah becomes a vamp and Jon, after accidentally killing a dog that had chased him to the photo booth, proves the theory that to take a photograph is not so much to take away a soul as to lay it bare. Gross introduces uncanny shifts in perspective as Jon describes his moment of surrender to the Facetaker.

> For a crazy moment it was as if the inside of my own skull *was* the camera – no, as if it was a darkened cinema and there was a tiny me in the back row, a kid who'd sneaked into an eighteen certificate film and found himself in there alone as the image of

my own face flashed up on the screen, huge, with a vacant look and staring eyes ... (110)

There were three faces – the last frame was a scorched black nothing – and they were looking at me, desperate, asking for something. They were alive, I knew; to throw them in the cart would be to kill them; they'd never forgive me. (111)

It shows you yourself, the parts you hide deep in your skull until *Flash!* they're looking at you face to face.

I could have said *No* at that moment, but I didn't. I couldn't stop now. Even if I didn't know if I was playing the game or if the game was playing me, I knew it had to go on. (112)

The terror in this book stems from its study of the influence which one inadequate human can exert over peers due to a disproportionate and misleading amount of charm. Jon, Sarah and Claire need only gentle encouragement from Denzil to take on grotesque new personae. The vague drugs-related horrors which Sarah's and Jon's parents imagine when they come home late are no more dangerous than the reality, that their teenagers are trapped in a particularly misguided fantasy directed by one of their number from which only their own enlightenment can save them.

Denzil is a magnet for his peers. He is a kind of dealer in the sense that everyone wants some of what he's got. Like Hugo in *Transformer*, he pounces on others' weaknesses and their desire to be among the élite, who are the only group allowed to exist in Denzil's universe. ('He saw people's soft spots as if they had targets painted on them' (8) ... 'If Denzil didn't think you were special, you were nothing' (32)). He is an unsettling influence on the girls, who compete for his attention, with Sarah abandoning notions of sisterhood in her resentment at being lumbered with the less popular Claire. When Jon tries to warn Sarah about the unpleasant facet of Denzil's personality she assumes that he is jealous, which in a way he is.

The Denzil that induces desire and envy only exists in his followers' imaginations and in the assumptions Jon makes, based on what little he knows about the classmate who keeps lesser mortals at arm's length: that Denzil has an enormous capacity for cruelty (the scene early in the book in which he orchestrates a teacher's mental breakdown is a psychological bloodbath); that he lies about most things; that he seems enviably self-contained and stylish. The reality of his home life – he has either run away from his parents or been abandoned by them and lives alone in a caravan – is the one thing he has not lied about, except by omission. However, as Jon begins to penetrate Denzil's façade, the gamemaster's private fantasy collapses even as elements of it are becoming real. Alice's *doppelgänger* has become flesh in the person of Mona, the mail-order bride of the local video shop owner, and Denzil's cool is no match for her husband's brawn. The game, too, is slipping out of his control as the stakes become higher. Desperate to restore his sense of self through the Facetaker, he tries and fails to sacrifice VI. His next almost-sacrifice is Jon, whom he hands over to VI to save his own skin. On the closing pages, Denzil and VI are killed by a train and Jon is left to live with the traumatic memory.

Throughout the novel Gross has kept the reader at a distance, watching the players being photographed, remodelled and costumed and sent out in character to perform on a restricted stage, returning constantly to the confined space of the photo booth. Towards the close of the story, with the Facetaker immobilised, he allows the reader to engage in a game on a wider playing field, as Jon follows Denzil and VI across the railway tracks. Still reeling from Denzil's betrayal, and believing death by approaching train to be moments away, Jon focuses on a detail of technology – 'Think of how a blender blade could look if you brought it up slowly, on full power, closer, closer, to half an inch from your eye' (180) – to spare himself and the reader the full experience of the accident. Gross rations out a teaspoonful of terror before stashing the rest of the gruesome details tantalisingly under wraps ('Try not to think about it', says Jon (180)). The momentum of the final two action-packed chapters sweeps young readers in and out of the potentially disturbing scene at speed.

Of Philip Gross's two villainous gamemasters, Denzil is less effective and has no long-term game plan of evil doings (Hugo has one which he carries out almost to the letter); but he is capable of surprising his jaded followers to the last. His *doppelgänger* story is proved to be true when his death supplies the sacrifice that switches Alice's body with Mona's. Minutes earlier, Jon had belatedly voiced his scepticism, explaining why gamemasters hold the influence they do. 'We swallowed it, me and Claire and Sarah, because oh, we wanted something special to happen' (173).

'Warmer, warmer, real warm' (176): *Paulina* by Lesley Howarth

The texts studied so far have focused on gamemasters who orchestrate group dynamics and individuals who drift in and out of the gamemasters' orbit. Lesley Howarth's horror novel *Paulina* (1999) features a solitary gamemaster who makes all the rules but cannot persuade anyone to play for long. Paulina McCoist, 'fourteen, blonde with brown eyes, tiny, sharp-boned and thin as a whip' (9) is a house ghost who died in the early 1980s, on the brink of a promising swimming career, after a fall down the basement steps.

Howarth is particularly skilled at depicting a certain type of character: the loner whose isolation is made more profound by special powers or by a driving obsession. For instance, MapHead can roam the globe at will but finds everyday family life closed to him; Thomas Moon in *Mister Spaceman* is fixated with becoming an astronaut and drifts around the galaxy inside his head, growing increasingly detached from Planet Earth. Paulina was a loner in life due to a combination of grim family circumstances and single-minded pursuit of championship status. Her father was an alcoholic who beat her mother and eventually blighted Paulina's career prospects. She had to learn discipline and self-reliance to protect herself and her younger brother, Davis, but longed for the carefree life of an ordinary well-loved teenager. On her last night alive, she let off steam by having a wild party, and died after a fall during a game of hide and seek. In death, she is left more severely alone, and seeks attention from the living through her disruptive behaviour. She rampages through her old home, breaking china and scattering rubbish around.

When the novel opens, the suburban house in Halifax, Connecticut, where Paulina and Davis hid while their estranged father hammered nightly on the door, belongs to a well-heeled couple, George and Annie. The life of Nine Maple Drive (an American Dream address) has moved on while Paulina's has not; there was no swimming pool in her day, when she needed one, but there is now. She does not feel at home in the new wing that George and Annie, keen renovators, have added to 'her' house. They are also keen home-swappers (in their eagerness, perhaps, to get a break from the quarters that the local teenagers know as Horror Central), and Paulina has attempted to tell her story to a succession of alarmed temporary visitors. She is in residence when Rebecca's family arrives from Cornwall. Howarth's opening sentences are invariably significant. This one reads: 'The pool's a lonely place by night, but it doesn't worry Paulina' (7).

The account which follows of Rebecca's holiday fortnight on Paulina's territory is a classic 'summer awakening' tale of loss of innocence, in a social rather than a sexual sense. When her holiday begins the English visitor is still clinging to childhood, although she sets great store by acting cool and favours adult pursuits such as shopping, sunbathing and doing her nails. She moves closer to adulthood through an increasing understanding of the events of Paulina's short, unhappy life, but first suffers the terrifying effects of the ghost's rage. The power struggle between Rebecca and Paulina, with the dead girl's misery, resentment and thirst for revenge pitted against her living contemporary's confusion, terror and eventual fury (on Paulina's behalf as well as generated by her), is the force that drives this gripping narrative.

Rebecca's family are innocents abroad who are seeking the classic New England adventure: whitewater tubing, Betty Crocker pancakes, rolling down the highway in the borrowed Buick, all of it captured on video. Her father longs to go on family hikes and discover New England heritage; Rebecca and her brother Bertie (the same age as Paulina's brother Davis) are more interested in the pool. On day one, Rebecca tours the Maple Drive house with the video camera, in the touching expectation that she will always delight in every detail, always want to look behind every door, in life as well as in the holiday home. Her voiceover will soon take on a *Blair Witch Project* quality. ('"This is the fridge." (Open fridge). "This is the living room. These are the stairs. This is the bedroom in the old part of the house. This is the bedroom in the new part of the house. And there – you can just see it out of the window – is the *swimming pool in the garden*"' (16).

Rebecca's dazzled encounter with the lifestyle of comfortably-off suburban New Englanders is overlaid with a moralistic tone ('it's the *lushest* house ... and the telly's huge ... and ... they are just ... living like *queens*' (16)). She perceives this sample of George and Annie's life as the typical North American experience, yet Paulina's mother brought her children up on welfare in a smaller, poorer incarnation of Nine Maple Drive. The luxurious aspects of George and Annie's home are a façade pasted over its unhappy history, and the joins show. In Annie's chintzy blue and white kitchen (out of character when compared with her messy office, for example) one of the New England homestyle doors conceals the less groomed part of the house, and the stairs pitch the unwary explorer headlong into the basement in the way that Pauline fell to her death.

The elusiveness of history, and the terrors presented by growing to understand it, are key themes in *Paulina*. Where David Almond's characters are sustained by their own history, Rebecca feels oppressed by too much of someone else's. She shuns the historical tourist attractions that entice her parents and is made uneasy by posters commemorating the Amistad rebellion and the American Indian experience, aspects of the history of the continent which often pass by the casual visitor. More troubling still is the relatively recent history of Paulina.

The ghost has left her mark all over the renovated house, where the air conditioning hums her name at night. Her presence is strongest in the walk-in closets in her bedroom, where she used to hide with Davis when Mr McCoist came calling, in the basement where she trains for swimming on Annie's exercise bike, and in the pool, built after her death by neighbour Maynard Freeman, who was in love with Mrs McCoist. After Paulina's fatal accident, Maynard gave his own new daughter her name (his wife had already called her Amy, and left the marriage shortly afterwards). While Rebecca pieces this most recent chapter of history together with trepidation, Paulina plays her games. She upstages the holidaymakers in their poolside sessions with the video camera, stuffs a dead bird into the pool filter and causes little accidents with the barbecue and the dreaded basement steps. Her most treasured possession, a plastic belt that her father gave her, serves to mark out her territory. Unwittingly, the hapless English invaders fuel her rage by swimming in her pool, pruning her favourite tree, cutting up her belt and simply enjoying themselves where she did not. Rebecca, whose life in the bosom of a loving family is a reminder of what was lacking in Paulina's adolescence, is a particular target and the ghost rifles through her clothes and hides her favourite pyjama case.

Rebecca's narrative voice is engaging: knowing, acerbic, breathlessly enthusiastic and wistful by turns. She wants the sort of American experience she knows from TV, one that is no more real than the 'history' packaged for tourists, and dreams of being friends with Maynard's daughter, Paulina (Lina) Freeman, who has cheerleader looks and delivers the paper. 'We could hang out together at the mall and do slow, regretful things like Angela in *My So Called Life* ... I wanted to be American. I wanted to meet someone cool' (32).

Lina, also in thrall to the dead Paulina, makes up the uneasy triangle of alliances and conflicts between the girls. She has grown up without a mother, and her much older father is obsessed with the memory of her namesake. Like Philip Gross's characters, she expresses her distress by trying on new identities, and she finds that the old McCoist home is 'the only place I can *be myself*'. She joins a gang who hold late-night poolside parties at number nine between and even during holiday lets. There she stays up late, swaps her preppie outfit for Goth gear, gets drunk and attempts to have sex in Paulina's old room with the boy who cleans the pool. 'Discover your other self, you know?' Lina tells Rebecca, as her friends throw corn chips in the water. 'Be what you wanna be' (78). Rebecca's grudging admiration for Lina ('By day she was Homecoming Queen, by night the Bride of Frankenstein. She partied wherever she wanted to. How cool and free was *that*?' (80)) is mingled with confusion at her new friend's switches of mood and image and with a surge of protectiveness towards Paulina: 'Why should *they* party in the place where she was so unhappy?' (80). Lina's final and most disturbing identity switch comes when, with the aid of some cheap 1980s fashions and hair colour, the brunette cheerleader appears on the doorstep of number nine in the guise of blonde and gaudily-dressed Paulina McCoist.

Rebecca's contempt for even recent history extends to unwise fashion statements that are dated rather than retro. She despises Paulina's precious belt as 'something left over from the eighties' and says of the gang who invade the garden with Lina 'They obviously got their clothes from the local Goth-U-Like catalogue ... How much more sad could they *be*?' (78). Paulina died around the time Rebecca was born; for Rebecca, to acknowledge Paulina's short, unhappy life means to contemplate an imaginative landscape fairly close to the world she inhabits now, but without her in it. The most chilling passage in the novel is one in which Paulina gives Rebecca the ultimate history lesson by showing her just such a landscape. Paulina has been drip-feeding details of her life and death by usurping Lina's paper round and delivering 1982 editions of the *Halifax Courant* to number nine. Trying to catch Paulina in the act, Rebecca realises that the dead girl is approaching down the Maple Drive of 1982. If Paulina has not yet died, that must mean Rebecca does not exist:

> I didn't have long to wait.
>
> The strangest feeling came over me, like the street was falling towards me. I got up and stood by the mailbox. My eyes watered. I felt very afraid. Every part of me trembled.
>
> The street looked different somehow, the houses older and fewer, the trees a lot smaller, the fences missing or gap-toothed. Even number nine looked stooped and smaller, and while I was noticing this my eyes were streaming with extreme fear and *someone was coming towards me.*
>
> I couldn't look directly at her for some reason. I tried to turn my head, but my eyes wouldn't focus. Out of the corner of my eye I was aware of her, though, even as my attention kept flashing on some really unimportant detail, like the grass at the edge of the kerb or the lace of my trainer or the mailbox. One moment she was at the end of the street; the next she was halfway down it. For some reason I noticed the cracks in the kerb; the next moment, I knew she was closer still; then it was the grass I was looking at; next moment *she was beside me*; oh no, BESIDE ME! and the side of my face felt like it was opening up and howling – howling – with fear. I flashed on my feet; SHE WAS STILL

THERE, OH, NO!, I flashed on my feet again, and the street was empty. (101)

Paulina's story is one of thwarted transformation both in life, when her father stopped her swimming in the state event after she had struggled to become county champion, and after death. Her efforts to communicate her history to each new set of visitors have been frustrating and futile. Lina and Rebecca unite to appease her spirit by offering her gifts, but only succeed when they unwittingly repeat history. Lina lures Rebecca into a party that follows the pattern of Paulina's last night, in which Rebecca repeats the circumstances of her death by falling down the basement stairs. Rebecca flies home having laid Paulina's ghost to rest. Lina's multiple transformations are likely to continue unless her father forsakes the dead girl for the living, but a quieter Paulina might be good for Lina too. In the last wild party game at Nine Maple Drive, the ghost finally finds someone to play with, and at least one of the players is still in 1982.

By some time after eleven we were playing some twisted version of Hide and Seek. There were no rules. No safety. Nothing familiar in the dark except a thrill of fear around every corner and sudden starts and rushes as whole rooms emptied and curtains squealed and somewhere a catcher stalked the house.
Stay quiet behind this curtain. Then you can cross the hall.
The game had gotten pretty wild since the lights had been put out. By now I was guided by her voice alone.
Warmer, warmer. Real warm.
Her voice ran continually in my head
Don't move yet! There's someone behind the door!
No matter where I went her voice was beside me in the dark.
OK, go! Through the living-room now!
This was the way Paulina had partied, the way she'd let off steam after so many months in a pressure-cooker, watched over by a drunk on the step. Her mom had gone out and her friends had come round. They'd also had the run of the house. They'd played Hide and Seek. Things had gotten pretty wild. *Davis, you there? Where are you?* (177)

Conclusion

The only enticement to play hide and seek is the dread certainty that you will be found. If the seeker wanders away in mid-game, the activity has no more appeal than John Askew's Death game in *Kit's Wilderness* without the watchers at the door ready to cry 'What was it like?' as the 'dead one' is restored to life in time for everyone to run home, shrieking, for baked beans and *Blue Peter*. To really relish being alone in the dark, you need to be with people who know what it's like.

The certainty cannot be more than 95 per cent: the player in hiding needs the added tension that comes with not knowing precisely when the seeker will look behind the curtain, or whether the dustballs under the bed will generate the sneeze that blows the game sky-high. Regular players of the game called Death knew that the outcome was predictable for most players most of the time; it was not only their fear of John Askew that kept them coming back, but also the knowledge that there were exceptions in their number (they knew about John, and soon there was Kit too). The same frisson can be supplied by the sense of a risk that the game might slip out of control; that the gamemaster, or the writer, might not have thought of everything; that there might be no overall game plan into which the apparently arbitrary decision of John Askew's spinning bottle fits.

Young readers' critical appreciation of horror fiction comes from the same root as their engagement in scary games: a mixture of dread, adrenaline and relief. They are most likely to engage with books in which they recognize part of themselves. Across the texts by Almond, Gross and Howarth considered here, there is a common theme of young protagonists who venture where adults do not dare to tread, meddling with the forbidden, the unspoken and the forgotten. In the course of this they discover previously unknown aspects of themselves, both encouraging (in the case of Michael, Kit and the Whitegates children in Almond's novels, and Emod in *Transformer*) and disturbing (Jon's latent cruelty in *Facetaker* and, more implicitly, Rebecca's growing sense of her own emotional fragility in *Paulina*, which manifests itself as a physical illness).

In this way, these novels reflect the condition of the young adolescent, whose life experience is often that of an incapacitated player in a game with no rulebook. Like all the texts discussed in this book, their readers' preoccupations include changes in the body, desire for acceptance by peers, growing awareness of death and loss as presences in their lives even if not as direct threats, and contemplation of their own human nature and their place in society. At this stage in their lives many adolescents feel that there is more uncertainty in their lives than is comfortable, so they turn to horror fiction with its 95 per cent certainties (the frightening content is 95 per cent on the page and someone else, the writer, is responsible for it) and 5 per cent spinning bottle factor, which is the effect of the story working in the reader's imagination. For 'certainties' we do not have to read 'predictability'. The content can encompass sophisticated scenarios and writing of the quality studied here. Within the certainty of an imaginary world constructed within limits and the expectation of a life-enhancing outcome, young readers are prepared to hand over responsibility for their place in the world to someone other than their parents. They are prepared to be frightened, to huddle in the dens that they have created, to hold their breath while the bottle spins, as long as they are led safely out again.

Bibliography

David Almond
Skellig (1998) London: Hodder Children's Books.
Kit's Wilderness (1999) London: Hodder Children's Books.
Heaven Eyes (2000) London: Hodder Children's Books.
Counting Stars (2000) London: Hodder Children's Books. (Published since the time of writing)

Melvin Burgess
Junk (1995) London: Andersen Press.

Philip Gross
Transformer (1996) London: Scholastic.
Psylicon Beach (1998) London: Scholastic.
Facetaker (1999) London: Scholastic.

Lesley Howarth
The Flower King (1993) London: Walker Books.
MapHead (1994) London: Walker Books.
Weather Eye (1995) London: Walker Books.
Mister Spaceman (1999) London: Walker Books.
Paulina (1999) London: Walker Books.

Notes

1   Writers' Awards 2000, Waterstone's and the Arts Council of England.
2   *The Daily Telegraph*, 14 March 2000.
3   Sarah Johnson, *The Times*, 20 January 2000.
4   Johnson, *op. cit.*

Bibliography

Appleyard, J. A. (1991) *Becoming a Reader: The Experience of Fiction from Childhood to Adulthood*. Cambridge: Cambridge University Press.

Auerbach, N. (1995) *Our Vampires, Ourselves*. London: University of Chicago Press.

Barker, M. (1984) *A Haunt of Fears: The Strange History of the British Horror Comics Campaign*. London: Pluto Press.

Baudrillard, J. (1993) *Symbolic Exchange and Death* (trans. I. Hamilton Grant). London: Sage.

Billen, A. (1996) 'Little horror'. *The Observer*, 6 October.

Billen, A. (1996) 'Little shocks for horrors'. *The Observer*, 25 February.

Bloom, C. (1993) *Creepers: British Horror and Fantasy in the Twentieth Century*. London: Pluto Press.

Carroll, N. (1990) *The Philosophy of Horror*. London: Routledge.

Charter, D. (1998) 'Top children's author makes chilling reading'. *The Times*, 26 August.

Clery, E. J. (1995) *The Rise of Supernatural Fiction 1762–1800*. Cambridge: Cambridge University Press.

Clover, C. (1992) *Men, Women and Chainsaws*. London: British Film Institute.

Craig, O. (1995) 'Horror and Aga sagas see romance off the shelves'. *The Sunday Times*, 3 December.

Cullingford, C. (1998) *Children's Literature and its Effects*. London and Washington: Cassell.

Feldman, S. (1994) 'Series of desire'. *Books for Keeps*, no. 84, pp. 20–1.

Fiske, J. (1989) *Reading the Popular*. London: Unwin Hyman.

Freud, S. (1978) *The Complete Psychological Works of Sigmund Freud*, vol. XVII (trans. J. Strachey). London: Hogarth Press.

Glover, D. (1996) *Vampires, Mummies, and Liberals: Bram Stoker and the Politics of Popular Fiction*. Durham: Duke University Press.

Grixti, J. (1989) *Terrors of Uncertainty: The Cultural Contexts of Horror Fiction*. London: Routledge.

Heller, T. (1987) *The Delights of Terror: An Aesthetics of the Tale of Terror*. Chicago: University of Illinois Press.

Hosking, S. and Schwerdt, D. (eds) (1999) *Extensions: Essays in English Studies from Shakespeare to the Spice Girls*. Adelaide: Wakefield Press.

Hunt, P. (1991) *Criticism, Theory, and Children's Literature*. Oxford: Blackwell.

Jackson, R. (1981) *Fantasy: The Literature of Subversion*. London and New York: Routledge.

King, S. (1991) *Danse Macabre*. London: Futura.

Kristeva, J. (1982) *Powers of Horror: An Essay on Abjection* (trans. L. S. Roudiez). New York: Columbia University Press.

McCarron, K. (1994) 'Point Horror and the Point of Horror', in A. Hogan (ed.) *Researching Children's Literature*. Southampton: LSU College of Higher Education.

Magistrol, T. and Morrison, M. (eds) (1996) *A Dark Night's Dreaming: Contemporary American Horror Fiction*. Columbia, South Carolina: University of South Carolina Press.

Pascal, F. (2000) *Fearless 1: Fearless*. London: Simon and Schuster.

Pascal, F. (2000) *Fearless 2: Sam*. London: Simon and Schuster.

Pascal, F. (2000) *Fearless 3: Run*. London: Simon and Schuster.

Pascal, F. (2000) *Fearless 4: Twisted*. London: Simon and Schuster.

Reynolds, K. *et al.* (1996) *Young People's Reading at the End of the Century*. London: Book Trust.

Riffaterre, H. (ed.) (1980) *The Occult in Language and Literature*. New York: New York Literary Forum.

St. John Barclay, G. (1978) *Anatomy of Horror: The Masters of Occult Fiction*. London: Weidenfeld and Nicolson.

Sarland, C. (1994) 'Attack of the Teenage Horrors: Theme and Meaning in Popular Series Fiction'. *Signal*, 73, pp. 48–61.

Sarland, C. (1991) *Young People Reading: Culture and Response*. Milton Keynes: Open University Press.

Showalter, E. (1997) *Hystories: Hysterical Epidemics and Modern Culture*. London: Picador.

Todorove, T. (1973) *The Fantastic: A Structural Approach to a Literary Genre* (trans. R. Howard). Cleveland and London: The Press Case of Western Reserve University.

Twitchell, J. B. (1985) *Dreadful Pleasures: An Anatomy of Modern Horror*. Oxford: Oxford University Press.

Vice, S. (ed.) (1993) *Beyond the Pleasure Dome: Writings and Addiction from the Romantics*. Sheffield: Sheffield Academic Press.

Warner, M. (1998) *No Go the Bogeyman: Scaring, Lulling, and Making Mock*. London: Chatto and Windus.

Index